TEACHING

IN THE NATIONAL CURRICULUM

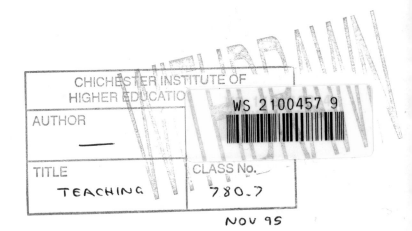

TEACHING

music

IN THE NATIONAL CURRICULUM

National Curriculum Music Working Group

EDITED BY

GEORGE PRATT & JOHN STEPHENS

Heinemann Educational Publishers
Halley Court, Jordan Hill, Oxford OX2 8EJ

MADRID ATHENS PARIS
FLORENCE PRAGUE WARSAW
PORTSMOUTH NH CHICAGO SAO PAULO
SINGAPORE TOKYO MELBOURNE AUCKLAND
IBADAN GABORONE JOHANNESBURG

First published 1995

99 98 97 96 95
10 9 8 7 6 5 4 3 2

British Library Cataloguing in Publication Data
A catalogue record for this book is available from the British Library
ISBN 0 435 81020 0

Designed by Roger Denning
Typeset by Books Unlimited (Nottm), Mansfield, Notts, NG19 7QZ
Cover design by Aricot Vert Design
Cover photograph by Pictor International
Printed and bound in Great Britain by Clays Ltd, St Ives plc

Contents

Members of the National Curriculum Music Working Group 1990–91

Sir John Manduell (Chairman)
John Stephens (Vice-Chair)
David Adams
Kevin Adams
Michael Batt
Michael Brewer
Philip Jones
Gillian Moore
George Pratt
Linda Read
Julian Smith
Christine Wood

Introduction

Sir John Manduell

All members of the National Curriculum Music Working Group would, I am confident, spontaneously agree that our work together was from start to finish invigorating and rewarding. The start itself could hardly have been more encouraging or propitious.

The resultant optimism initially flowed directly from the circumstances in which we were to be brought together. To the delight of many, the Department of Education and Science (as the present Department for Education was then styled) had decided that music should be one of the National Curriculum subjects. Along with art and physical education, music had secured one of the last three places in the team, following the selection of seven important subjects such as English and maths – and an eighth, Welsh, in Wales – rightly regarded as indispensable.

Together we formed an interesting triumvirate to complete the batting order. One of the earliest questions we began asking ourselves was how far the three might need or want to work together. After all, it had been decided, for example, that formulating recommendations for dance was to fall to the physical education team, but had not dance some association with music? Above all it seemed to all of us that more positive results could follow if we kept in touch, and so it was that from time to time I found myself discussing matters of common concern with the chairmen of these two groups: Ian Beer for physical education and Lord Renfrew for art. Harrow and Jesus College, Cambridge – a formidable combination.

Kenneth Baker was Secretary of State at the time when the members of our group were appointed and when we started our work. Angela Rumbold was Minister of State and, guided by officers, was centrally responsible for picking and assembling our team. The fact that little more than a dozen moons on we were offering our final thoughts to Kenneth Clarke as Secretary of State, and that we had for a brief period served John MacGregor in that office in the interim, reflects as much the speed of politics as the industry with which we applied ourselves to our tasks.

In approaching those tasks – and, indeed, in the complex and **vii** concentrated process of wrestling with them – we owed an enormous debt to the comprehensive and resilient support we consistently received from the officers delegated to work with us. Together they were a dedicated team without whom we could never have approached the results we believe we ultimately achieved and without whom our deliberations would have been both much more erratic and far less entertaining than was in fact the case. If this introduction only expresses our appreciation and gratitude towards some of them by name, they and their erstwhile colleagues should be well aware that we recognize our indebtedness to all of them.

To three of those splendid colleagues we owe a significant debt. In Leon Crickmore, then HMI Staff Inspector in Music, we enjoyed the support of a man whose wisdom derived from long and wide-ranging experience and whose priorities were consistently directed towards the twin concerns of the art and the pupil. It is to our good fortune that Leon is today a widely respected consultant whose energies and judicious advice continue to be applied in serving the greater good of both music and education.

To Barney Baker we could – and repeatedly did – turn for authoritative advice on how we should best crack a particular procedural nut. Barney's advice derived from distinguished senior service in the Department, an experience which enabled him to provide invaluable guidance and wisdom, all of which he imparted with a touch of engaging irreverence which brought a welcome measure of colour and good humour to our proceedings.

In Sheena Evans we enjoyed a measure of support which, because it was founded upon an exuberant enthusiasm for the task in hand, provided us all with a steady stream of invaluable encouragement. Enthusiastic Sheena may have been; she was also tirelessly energetic and impressively efficient. No task was too much for her, as was well illustrated when on one occasion during the early days, as we were preparing our initial working arrangements but when I was tied up on an assignment in Cumbria, Sheena simply solved the problem by darting up to Windermere by train to meet me.

No chairman of an ad hoc group charged with such considerable responsibilities could possibly have hoped for a more dedicated or loyal team than that which I was privileged to lead through the complex exercise whose character and conclusions are developed in the ensuing chapters. Being the co-authors of this book their contributions will speak for themselves. Being the co-authors of the results we ultimately achieved – results happily now confirmed and established for years to come as a result of the admirable conclusions reached in Sir Ron Dearing's report – these collective achievements will, I am confident, similarly speak for themselves.

It is thus neither appropriate nor desirable that I should seek to elaborate upon their individual contributions, for each member of the team had so many different roles accorded to her or him that it would be quite impossible to do justice to those varied responsibilities within a short introductory chapter such as this. At different times each member of the team could be called upon to carry through an individual assignment or to be part of a sub-group concentrating on a specific topic or, again, to play a part in the collective endeavours of the whole team. All were repeatedly called upon to undertake research and to compile detailed conclusions. All were frequently asked to dedicate whole week-ends to our work, to engage in day-long and day–night meetings and to travel considerable distances. All willingly responded, as they did when making wide-ranging visits to view work in schools up and down the land or, for that matter, to assess practice abroad.

Such forays could bring their lighter moments. I suspect that all members of the team will recall what befell us one cold night in early March when we had undertaken a working weekend at a country hotel in Wales. While otherwise comfortable, the hotel proved to have a self-motivated fire alarm system, although we were unaware of this when we were tipped shivering in our pyjamas onto a frosty lawn at four in the morning. It was perhaps inevitable that after the alarm was declared over it would take some time before circulation in frozen limbs could be restored sufficiently to enable sleep to be resumed. In my case I seemed only just to have got back to sleep when there was an insistent knocking at the door. Without stood a small (seemingly shivering) Welshman in an old macintosh, who handed me a sheet of paper. This told residents that the management regretted having woken guests for no reason. The author of the document seemed impervious to the fact that he had compounded the disaster by arranging for immediate circulation by hand of this apology. If ever, as chairman, I was able to render a service to my colleagues it was by firmly admonishing the innocent messenger that only on pain of eternal retribution would he present further copies of this document before breakfast time.

I have said that I would not be attempting to refer to members of our team individually, but there must be two exceptions, for it is due very largely to the skill and resolution of two colleagues that we can attribute the existence of this book. It is John Stephens, my vice-chairman, who entertained the original concept that we should collaborate to publish it, and called us all to reassemble for a weekend conference to plan its structure and content. Professor George Pratt has encouraged and cajoled us to complete our respective contributions against a very tight time-scale, and has subsequently collated and edited them for publication. All of us share their hope that, by making our experiences available both for the general reader and for those professionally concerned, from **ix** primary schoolteachers to music specialists, this book will be of real and practical benefit and that, thereby, music in our schools may be helped to prosper.

Sir John Manduell CBE
Chairman
National Curriculum Music Working Group and Music Forum

Editors' Introduction

George Pratt and John Stephens

The achievements of teachers have transformed the music curriculum in schools. Within a couple of generations the focus of musical activities in classrooms has developed dramatically from listening to gramophone records, learning the rudiments of music theory and singing a few songs, to practical experiences and encounters with music as performers, composers and listeners. Without these years of curriculum development and the dedication of teachers and musicians to improving the quality of pupils' musical education, music might well not have been incorporated as a foundation subject into the National Curriculum in England and Wales.

While it was one of the last subjects to be dealt with in the detail of the curriculum, it proved to be one which evoked an exceptional level of interest and attention from parents, professional musicians and politicians. The common factor in each of these groups is their aspirations for the pupils.

Given the right opportunities, encouragement and skilful teaching we know that pupils respond and can perform with confidence, compose with imagination, listen and appraise with understanding.

The law, that is the statutes relating to the National Curriculum, provide a framework within which teachers' judgements and skills can be exercised. The transmission of the curriculum is in the hands of teachers, for whose aspirations for quality this book is addressed. It has grown from the experience and deliberations of the members of the National Curriculum Music Working Group which, at its final meeting, undertook to explore ways to continue to contribute to the debate about the nature, scope and delivery of music in schools.

A generous donation from the Pilgrim Trust facilitated further meetings of sub-groups within the Working Party and one full meeting to discuss the present handbook. It represents a continuation and extension of the advice offered to the Secretaries of State in August 1991. Whilst it has no official status and is unlikely to be the basis of any statutory instrument, it represents the collective views of twelve professionals whose experience in the field of music education is varied, diverse and comprehensive.

The Music Forum, as it has retitled itself, set out to fulfil two tasks. The first was to produce a short video programme to support training initiatives for teachers of pupils at Key Stage 2. This has been achieved and copies distributed without charge to all local education authorities, and also to colleges which train students to teach in primary schools. The second task set by the Music Forum was to produce this handbook.

Individuals and groups from within the whole Music Forum have contributed to the separate chapters of this handbook, whilst the connections between them have been our responsibility as editors.

The Forum has, of course, taken account of events subsequent to the initial formulation of the music curriculum. We have followed developments in the organisation and funding of the education service, the consultation on the revised requirements for the National Curriculum and the publication of the latest statutory Order for music in January 1995. The Forum has also drawn upon its direct experience of music education which collectively and individually spans the range from infants to students in higher education as teachers, advisers, inspectors, organizers and administrators; composers, performers and representation from the commercial world and publishing.

The motivation which drove this group during its initial task of making recommendations for official and public consideration, has sustained members' active interest during the production of the present handbook. We want to articulate, as precisely as possible, what is necessary for a rich musical education for young people; the development of potential through skills, knowledge and understanding, an enjoyment and above all a love of music.

We could not, though, have written this book from our own experience alone. Sir John Manduell, in his introduction, has acknowledged the invaluable contributions of others to the final report of the Music Working Group, Music for ages 5 to 14 (Department of Education and Science and the Welsh Office, August 1991). We in turn owe thanks to those who have made it possible to produce this book. Our publishers Heinemann Educational, and our commissioning editor Sue Walton, have responded with remarkable alacrity to the exceptional circumstances in which we found ourselves. The Music Working Group had gained a uniquely rich experience during our year's work together. We had distilled the wisdom and advice of hundreds of respondents to a public advertisement to write to the Group, and we had subsequently watched developments as the National Curriculum Council and the Welsh Office turned our hundred-page report into a nine-page curriculum.

In such a (necessary) process of distillation, much valuable detail is inevitably lost, and it is that which we wanted to preserve and share with colleagues in the teaching profession, and indeed in the wider world of music as a whole. We could not sensibly do so, however, until Sir Ron Dearing had led his review of the whole National Curriculum, including music. We have very much admired the process of this review and the exceptionally valuable input by the School Curriculum and Assessment Authority, its working groups and its officers led by Tony Knight. The fruits of this exercise have now been accepted and made law. This happened in January of this year (1995) and our publishers Heinemann Educational have achieved little short of a miracle to have this book available well before the beginning of the first school year for which the revised curriculum is a legal requirement.

The headteachers of Prior Weston School, London and Kingsdale School, Dulwich, kindly gave their consent for photographs to be taken of pupils and teachers in their schools. The Music Forum commissioned Edward Park to take the photographs.

We owe a great debt to Elaine Hardy who turned much of the material from hand-written notes or amateur typing into a word-processed basis for further editing.

Most of all, we want to acknowledge the wisdom and inspiration of musicians and music educators over the last three decades – those who responded to the Music Working Group, those who have continued the process of evolution from our initial proposals, and those who have influenced our thinking in less direct ways. Music education has undergone nothing short of a revolution since the 1960s. It is fascinating to speculate on what the effects will be, a decade from now, of a school population emerging into adulthood, all of whom, in state education at least, will have experienced performing, composing, listening and appraising from the age of five.

1 The National Curriculum for music

John Stephens

Music is a foundation subject in the National Curriculum in England and Wales. The Education Reform Act 1988 placed a responsibility upon the Secretaries of State to establish this curriculum by specifying, in an Order, appropriate Attainment Targets, Programmes of Study and assessment arrangements for each of the foundation and core subjects.

The Music Working Group

To advise on the detail of the targets and Programmes of Study the Secretaries of State for Education and Science, and for Wales, invited a number of people interested and experienced in each specialist field to submit proposals for consideration. The Music Working Group was set up on 4 July 1990 with terms of reference which stated that

> because of the nature of the subject, the objectives (Attainment Targets) and means of achieving them (Programmes of Study) should not be prescribed in as much detail for music as for the core and other foundation subjects ... schools and teachers should have substantial scope to develop their own schemes of work.

The brief given to the twelve members of the Music Working Group was to advise on a statutory framework which was sufficiently broad and flexible to allow schools wide discretion in relation to the matters to be studied.

The Group met under the chairmanship of Sir John Manduell and produced an interim report which was delivered to the Secretaries of State on 21 December 1990. This was subsequently published to provide a basis for consultation and discussion.

Both the interim report and the accompanying letter from the Secretary of State for Education and Science stimulated a wide public debate and discussion about the nature and scope of music studies in schools. Over 700 responses were received, many of them in turn from organisations representing the views of large numbers of music teachers, professional musicians and, significantly, parents. A full list was included, at the insistence of Sir John Manduell, as Annex H of our final report (Music for ages 5 to 14, DES and Welsh Office, August 1991).

The Working Group proceeded with its task of formulating advice for the Secretaries of State during the first six months of 1991, submitting its final report on 28 June.

Revision

In April 1993 the then Secretary of State invited Sir Ron Dearing to undertake a review of the National Curriculum and the structures for assessment. The Curriculum Council for Wales was invited to undertake a parallel review.

A consultation period and subsequent review followed in early 1994 with support from advisory groups, including one for music. Proposals for revised Orders were launched for further consultation in May 1994.

This period for consultation provided an opportunity for further refinement and clarification. A report on the 1994 consultation (School Curriculum and Assessment Authority, 1994), indicated that this process had helped to focus attention on the relationships between the 'Programmes of Study' – the framework for schools to construct their schemes of work – and the 'End of Key Stage Statements' – the yardstick for measuring pupils' achievement. The result was a marked shift in emphasis, from assessment to teaching. The report comments that

> schools should use their professional judgement to create schemes of work which are based on the Programmes of Study and which incorporate plans for teaching and everyday assessment in ways that are appropriate to the school and its pupils.

The End of Key Stage Statements were replaced by End of Key Stage Descriptions, providing in continuous prose a guide to the criteria for assessing pupils at the ages of seven, eleven and fourteen.

The music curriculum

People of every culture have found a need to express and share feelings, thoughts and ideas by ordering sounds into forms which symbolize and interpret their experience. The creation of music stems from our need to communicate through patterns of sounds which have significance, and which may be re-created on subsequent occasions.

Music is so much a part of the background of everyday life that it tends to be taken for granted. Yet, for many people it is a powerful focus for creative energy, and one which both stimulates and guides the imagination. Music education aims to develop aesthetic sensitivity and creative ability in all pupils.

The curriculum is taken to mean 'that which schools intend their pupils shall learn and experience'. It is important to recognize that this is not a matter of chance encounter, but rather a planned and considered path towards the achievement of skills, knowledge and understanding.

The music curriculum interprets this description in relation to the basic activities relating to musical experience, namely performing, composing, and listening and appraising.

The development of musical perception and skills is dependent upon the quality, range and appropriateness of these musical experiences, as they are provided within and outside school. There are many different styles of music appropriate for different purposes and offering different kinds of satisfaction and challenge; excellence may be found in any style of musical expression.

The study of music as a foundation subject provides for the progressive development of:

- awareness and appreciation of organized sound patterns
- skills in movement (such as motor co-ordination and dexterity), vocal skills, and skills in aural imagery (imagining and internalising sounds), acquired through exploring and organizing sound
- sensitive, analytical and critical responses to music
- the capacity to express ideas, thoughts and feelings through music
- awareness and understanding of traditions, idioms and musical styles from a variety of cultures, times and places
- the experience of fulfilment which derives from striving for the highest possible artistic and technical standards.

Statutory Orders

The statutory Orders (for England and Wales) set out Attainment Targets and Programmes of Study. Published in March 1992, and revised in the spring of 1995, these apply to all maintained (including grant-maintained) schools in England and Wales. Whilst not being required by statute to deliver a music curriculum, many independent schools also find the structures helpful in planning a scheme and assessing pupils' progress. The statutory requirements provide a framework within which schools have a wide discretion in the content, repertoire and means of delivery. The structure, provided by the Orders and now familiar to many teachers, is defined within **Programmes of Study** and **End of Key Stage Descriptions**.

The Programmes of Study comprise the matters, skills and processes which pupils need to be taught and experience to enable them to meet the objectives set out in the Attainment Targets. They are not, as was misunderstood by some readers of the Music Working Group's Interim Report, schemes of work which detail lesson content and repertoire.

The important task of planning for the delivery of the music curricu- **3** lum is supported by the statutory Programmes of Study which are set out to meet the objectives for each **Key Stage**; that is for Key Stage 1, pupils aged five to seven years; for Key Stage 2, pupils aged seven to eleven years; and for Key Stage 3, pupils aged eleven to fourteen years. Key Stage 4, pupils aged fourteen to sixteen years, is not included in the statutory regulations, although it is recognized that schools will wish to provide opportunities for those pupils who wish to continue their studies at this stage, often by undertaking an examination course within the General Certificate of Secondary Education (GCSE).

The Programmes of Study are now helpfully set out in straightforward language defining at each Key Stage what pupils should be taught and, in the curriculum for England, the opportunities that should be provided. This is preceded by common requirements.

At the end of each Key Stage, namely at the ages of seven, eleven and fourteen, teachers may make assessments of pupils' musical development; the skills, knowledge and understanding which pupils of different abilities and maturities can be expected to achieve. The criteria for making these assessments are incorporated into the statutory Orders as **End of Key Stage Descriptions**.

Unlike core subjects such as English, mathematics and science, and some of the foundation subjects in the National Curriculum, it is not intended that there will be national standardized tests to make these assessments.

Attainment targets defined in the National Curriculum identify the skills, knowledge and understanding expected of pupils in each subject. For schools in England these are grouped under the headings:

- Performing and Composing
- Listening and Appraising.

In the course of discussions following the publication of the National Curriculum Council Consultation Report (January 1992), it was suggested that the first of these should be given twice the weighting of the second. However, when the statutory Order for England was published, no such weighting was specified for the 1992 Curriculum. In the revised Order of 1995, the weighting is still not stated but clearly implied by the content and layout of the curriculum. 'Pupils should be given opportunities to' engage in four fields of activity relating to Performing and Composing but to only two relating to Listening and Appraising. Similarly, the list of what 'pupils should be taught' contains eight matters within Performing and Composing but only five in Listening and Appraising. This reflects the views of all of us concerned with the original proposals, and most of those who advised us – that there are three ways in which we engage in music: composing it, performing it, and listening critically (appraising it) – and all are equally important.

They can be identified and defined discretely, in isolation from each other, but all three fields of musical activity should receive approximately equal attention and be integrated holistically, each affecting and influencing the other.

The revised Order clearly implies this equal weighting of the three musical activities, but also reflects the concern of Sir Ron Dearing that there should be no prescription in the demands of the curriculum. The responsibility therefore rests with teachers responding to the particular demands and circumstances of their pupils.

The Order for Wales identified the three activities in music as separate Attainment Targets, and they remain so in the revised 1995 Curriculum. They are:

- Performing
- Composing
- Appraising.

Implementing the National Curriculum

Most schools already offered a music programme to pupils, so the introduction of the National Curriculum for music required only a check that the necessary statutory elements were being covered. However, because the statutory curriculum has been applied progressively – one cohort of pupils at each Key Stage, commencing on 1 August 1992 and in subsequent years – the following pattern has emerged.

Key Stage 1 – five to seven year olds

1992 Year 1 (five year olds)
1993 Years 1 and 2 (five and six year olds)
1994 First End of Key Stage Description (end of Key Stage 1)

Key Stage 2 – seven to eleven year olds

1992 Year 3 (seven year olds)
1993 Years 3 and 4 (seven and eight year olds)
1994 Years 3, 4 and 5 (seven, eight and nine year olds)
1995 Years 3, 4, 5 and 6 (seven, eight, nine and ten year olds)
1996 First End of Key Stage Description (end of Key Stage 2)

Key Stage 3 — eleven to fourteen year olds

1992 Year 7 (eleven year olds)
1993 Years 7 and 8 (eleven and twelve year olds)
1994 Years 7, 8 and 9 (eleven, twelve and thirteen year olds)
1995 First End of Key Stage Description (end of Key Stage 3)

So, a temporary problem arises during this staged introduction of the curriculum that, in some areas at Key Stages 2 and 3, pupils may not have covered the work and developed the competencies from the earlier stages. It continues to be necessary to take account of this when planning for the initial implementation of the National Curriculum.

HM Inspectors visited a large number of schools during the first year of the implementation of the National Curriculum (1992–93) and reported on their findings in Music — Key Stage 1, 2 and 3 (published by the Office for Standards in Education ISBN 0-11-350034-3). Four of the eight issues identified in this report relate, at Key Stages 1 and 2, to access and planning. They stress the need to review and revise schemes of work; to ensure, through planning, the achievements of progression in learning; and to widen the styles of music addressed. The message of progression is sustained in the report's references to Key Stage 3 where HM Inspectors stressed the need to build better curricular links with feeder schools and increase teachers' expectations of new pupils to the secondary school.

Planning

The inclusion of music in the National Curriculum offers a framework for all schools to plan, assess and evaluate their programme of music activities. The legal requirements are not an inhibiting factor; they allow considerable flexibility. A detailed consideration of planning is to be found in chapter 3.

In devising a coherent policy for the music curriculum it is important to take account of the relationships between its various components. These may well be delivered in various ways — by class teachers and in some cases by professional musicians who are not class teachers. Instrumental teachers need to be fully aware of the point their pupils have reached in following the general music curriculum, of the detailed scheme of work involved, and of the tasks and materials used in the classroom. In turn, the instrumental music lessons need to be regarded as an alternative form of delivery, not as an adjunct or optional extra. Schools will need to take account of local circumstances, the availability of specialist instrumental teachers, the wishes of parents and the needs of pupils in determining the range and nature of their instrumental provision.

Revised curriculum Order (1995)

The revised Order provides welcome clarity and simplification in the language used and the layout of both Programmes of Study and End of Key Stage Descriptions. The relationship between the delivery of the curriculum and the assessment of pupils' progress is clearer. The English Order is headed by a statement requiring that

> pupils' understanding and enjoyment of music should be developed through activities that bring together requirements from both Performing and Composing, and Listening and Appraising wherever possible.

This exhortation to a holistic approach is also found in the Welsh Order, and is very welcome. The separation of musical activity into apparently discrete fields – performing, composing, listening and appraising – might encourage a compartmentalized approach to teaching and learning. We will stress again in chapter 2 the integrated nature of musical activity. We cannot perform effectively without appraising what we are doing; decision-making in composing is an aspect of appraising; music is composed to be performed – and so on.

The End of Key Stage Descriptions also recognize that music is a practical activity and that pupils' understanding and enjoyment should be developed through a coherent and holistic approach to the discrete activities of performing, composing, listening and appraising.

Whilst the Order does not prescribe teaching methods or strategies it indicates that, at every Key Stage, pupils should be given opportunities to use sounds and respond to music as individuals, in pairs, in groups and as a class. The corporate nature of music making is thus underlined and the wide range of activities in curriculum and extended-curriculum opportunities are embraced by the National Curriculum.

The elements of music are restored, in the revised Orders, to their rightful place at the head of the whole curriculum. The Music Forum regretted that, in the revisions following the final report it presented (as the Music Working Group), these elements were placed in the 1992 Orders in such a way that they appeared to relate only to Listening and Appraising, tempting readers to overlook that they are the analytical basis of Performing and Composing too.

The elements are defined for each Key Stage, providing a perspective of progression in the development of skills and concepts. Thus recognising high/low, an aspect of pitch at Key Stage 1, becomes distinguishing gradations of pitch at Key Stage 2 and discriminating various scales and modes at Key Stage 3. Inevitably, in such a concise document – the whole English curriculum can be fitted onto one side of an A3 page – concepts are expressed very tersely and need to be unwrapped. Teachers will recognize that 'higher than -' and 'lower than -' precedes the recognition of high sounds and low sounds, implied in Key Stage 1. The important point which survives the brevity of the published Order is that progression is clearly signalled.

The repertoire chosen for performing and listening also indicates incremental development, using such phrases as 'extend pupils' musical experience' and 'develop appreciation' (England) and 'be progressively more demanding' (Wales). At Key Stage 1 in the English Order this is simply defined as music from a variety of styles from different times and cultures, and by well-known composers and performers, past and present. At Key Stage 3 the specification retains the original recommendation, i.e. music in a variety of styles:

- from the European 'classical' tradition from its earliest roots to the present day
- from folk and popular music
- from countries and regions of the British Isles
- from cultures across the world
- by well-known composers and performers, past and present.

These categories have already been introduced as examples of a varied repertoire at Key Stage 2.

The Welsh curriculum invites a similar variety, together with specific reference to the music of Wales.

The detail of the revisions to the Programmes of Study and End of Key Stage Descriptions is considered in chapters 2 and 3.

2 Performing; composing; listening and appraising

George Pratt

The title of this chapter springs from the three musical activities named in the Attainment Targets of the curriculum.

Attainment targets

Music in the National Curriculum (England) identifies two Attainment Targets:
AT 1 : Performing and Composing
AT 2 : Listening and Appraising.
Music in the National Curriculum (Wales) identifies three Attainment Targets:
AT 1 : Performing
AT 2 : Composing
AT 3 : Appraising.
A significant change in the revised Order for England (1995) is that the words 'Attainment Target' do not appear in the Programmes of Study but only in the End of Key Stage Descriptions. This change is a clear and welcome indication of the essential difference between the delivery of the curriculum in teaching and learning on the one hand, and the need, from time to time, to make **summative** assessments of pupils – identifying their current achievements – for the purpose of reporting to parents, to headteachers and governors, and not least to pupils themselves. So the End of Key Stage Descriptions with their Attainment Targets are instruments of summative assessment; the musical activities in the Programmes of Study which constitute the body of the curriculum on the other hand are the means whereby the curriculum is delivered, and assessed formatively on a day-to-day basis.

Of course, there is a need to make **formative** assessments – identifying what may next be done to build on present achievement – by both teachers and pupils as part of the teaching/learning process. This is essential to ensure progression. All concerned need constantly to monitor progress, and to determine what the next stage should be. This is dealt with further in chapter 6.

Definitions

Whatever assessment structure may be imposed by legal statute, there remain three musical activities in which people engage:

Performing

Summary
- The performing **repertoire** includes pupils' own music and the music of others which they will learn.
- The **media** for performing include pupils' voices, sounds they make with their bodies such as clapping, sound sources they discover around them, simple untuned and tuned classroom instruments, more sophisticated instruments of various ethnic origins such as recorders, Western orchestral instruments, sitar and tabla, steel pans and gamelan orchestras.
- The **range** of performing experiences is from informal demonstrations of discovered sounds by one pupil to one or a few others; through more formal prepared performances by several to the whole class or by one whole class to another; to staged performances, planned and rehearsed for presentation to audiences within the school or outside in the local community.

Performing, whether by singing or playing an instrument, is one of the two principal means (with composing) of developing and sharing musical skills, creativity and understanding. By performing their own and other people's compositions, pupils will develop their skills of listening, singing and playing. They will also learn to present a programme to an audience – an important aspect of shared musical experience. Although music can often be enjoyed alone, by playing in isolation or listening to recordings for instance, it can easily become impoverished and stagnant if musical experiences and enthusiasms are not communicated and shared with others.

In pupils' early years at school, performing will include moving rhythmically to music; clapping in time to it; humming or chanting; taking part in musical games; and singing from memory. As pupils gain in manual dexterity, vocal range and musical understanding, they will be able to perform an ever-increasing repertoire, and to develop the skills needed to play by ear on a variety of instruments, including electronic instruments; to sing part songs; to sing and play from signs, symbols and cues their own music and the compositions of others; to direct and be directed in performance; and to present performances to other people.

Performing their own compositions

Chapter 7 includes a comprehensive survey of music selected and composed to meet the various needs of teachers and pupils at each Key Stage.

Composing

Summary
- 'Composing' refers to three levels of activity: spontaneous musical creation through **improvising**; **refining** original ideas to a finished state; altering and adapting existing music by **arranging** it.
- An expected outcome of composing should be performing the resulting music, both in the various stages of its development and in its finished state.
- Compositions should be stored by means of recording, signs, symbols or cues, or conventional notations as appropriate.

Composing is now well established and accepted as a valid means of self-expression, not only for those who aspire to greatness in the field but for everyone. The value of composing lies in the development not only of pupils' own musical creativity, but also of their ability to appreciate and evaluate the compositions of other people: the process of composing is a valuable aid to the development of our musical understanding. By tackling and solving problems in their own compo-   **11** sitions, pupils come to appreciate the problems and their solutions in the music both of other pupils and also of established composers.

The task of composing will lead, with appropriate guidance from teachers, to pupils thinking carefully about the elements which they wish to use, identified in the National Curriculum as pitch, duration, dynamics, tempo, timbre, texture and structure. It will involve them in thinking about the use of particular musical conventions and the ways in which composers have used sounds and structures for particular effects and purposes. It will also lead them to consider the best way of recording or notating their music, and enable them to listen with enhanced perceptiveness to the ways in which established composers use those same musical elements.

The curriculum refers to three kinds of composing:

- **improvising** – creating music by spontaneous performance
- **composing** – evaluating and revising initial musical ideas, and storing them for subsequent recall
- **arranging** – adapting a given piece of music.

Composing will include exploring sounds from a wide range of sources such as body sounds like clapping, to vocal sounds and instruments of varying levels of sophistication. Exploration can be gradually extended and developed to include choosing, combining and ordering sounds, inventing and using rhythmic and melodic patterns, and taking decisions on structure and form as well as elements such as pitch and tempo. At the higher levels of attainment, pupils will have gained a clear idea about the character, mood and idiom – a recognisably personal utterance – of their improvisations, compositions and arrangements, and develop the ability to control and manipulate musical materials and ideas in increasingly imaginative and expressive ways.

It is axiomatic and essential that pupils' compositions should be performed. Their own critical awareness is often greatly heightened when other people listen to their music and, without performance of it, the function of music as a means of communication will be lost.

The National Curriculum places some emphasis on the need for pupils gradually to learn techniques and conventions for storing the improvisations, compositions and arrangements they undertake. In the English curriculum, these include:

- at Key Stage 1
  symbol – that which by convention or agreement represents something else; for example an object chosen to represent a sound pattern, a graphic score, staff notation

Exploring sounds from a range of sources

- at Key Stage 2
  notation(s) – any means of writing down music so that it can be saved and performed, is added
- at Key Stage 3
  notation(s) – specifically including conventional staff notation, and the ability to use recording equipment where appropriate, is added.

The 1992 curriculum included two other means of storing and communicating music and they are worth noting here as complementary to, and even implicit in, the concise wording of the 1995 revised Order. They are:

- signs – gestures or written marks expressing a meaning; e.g. the hand gestures of a conductor, the word 'crescendo' or the abbreviation 'p'
- cues – audible or written indications of musical events to which a performer is to respond.

Listening and appraising

Summary
- 'Appraising' refers to attentive listening, internalising, recalling and critical evaluation of music both as sheer sound and also in so far as it reflects, and is a reflection of, its historical and cultural contexts.
- Effective appraising requires the knowledge, perception and understanding of musical elements together with relevant factual knowledge.

The repertoire available for appraising (English Order) includes all the areas listed in the Curriculum beginning at Key Stage 1 with music from different times and cultures and by well known composers and performers (past and present) and extending, by Key Stage 3, to five categories of music:

- from the European 'classical' tradition, from its earliest roots to the present day
- from folk and popular music
- from the countries and regions of the British Isles
- from cultures across the world
- by well known composers and performers, past and present.

The first four of these categories were coined by the original Music Working Group who agonized for a long time over the word 'classical', conscious of its more specific use to describe a limited period of musical style. Members of the Group finally salved their consciences by putting the word into inverted commas – and so it has remained.

The Programmes of Study in the revised Order add a very welcome further category, that of '[pupils'] own and others' compositions and performances', demonstrating that 'listening and appraising' has now been unequivocally extended to include music newly composed and performed by pupils as well as the vast heritage of other people's music from a millennium or more of human culture across the world.

Unlike 'performing' and 'composing', both well established terms in music curricula and syllabuses, 'appraising' is a less familiar word, selected to include not only hearing music and paying attention to it, but also internalising it for subsequent recall, and the whole aesthetic dimension of interpretation and evaluation.

When the word first entered the curriculum in 1992, it was often misunderstood. A research project in the RAMP (Research into Applied Musical Perception) Unit at the University of Huddersfield has since been concerned with investigating the meaning and implications of the word, and how it can be applied in practice. In this as yet unpublished enquiry, the Research Fellow running the project has identified three particular areas of confusion:

- Some teachers have believed 'appraising' to be a form of assessment, to discover if pupils can carry out a particular musical activity. In fact, it involves pupils assessing themselves, as will be made clear by the explanation of 'areas of appraising' below.
- Others believed that 'appraising' involves the acquisition of factual knowledge-based information about music. This is true where such knowledge is relevant to the music itself, and enhances understanding of it. To have a heightened enjoyment of a virtuoso piece through knowing the difficulties of the techniques involved is appraising. But to know the date of the composer's birth is much less likely to be directly relevant to the musical experience. The revised Order constantly implies that whatever the information acquired, it should be directly relevant to the music pupils are composing, performing and listening to. The team of teachers participating in the RAMP research also believes that as far as possible this information should be acquired in an experiential way.
- Thirdly, some have explained 'appraising' as listening to music and talking about it. While this is certainly a component of the curriculum, identified in the Programmes of Study by expressions like 'describe in simple terms', 'express ideas and opinions ... developing a musical vocabulary' and 'express and justify opinions and preferences', it is essential to recognize that pupils can often more easily demonstrate what they hear in music than talk about it – and that this, too, is 'appraising'.

The RAMP research has led a group of practising teachers to identify nine 'areas' within which appraising occurs. Pupils are appraising music when they:

- listen to music for a particular purpose.
  The members of the Music Forum have a memorable personal experience to illustrate this. An argument had occurred before a concert about whether Beethoven's Violin Concerto begins with four or five strokes on the timpani. After heated discussion, and without a score to resolve the dispute, the members could not possibly have 'appraised' more intently the first 4/4 bar – and one further beat, in fact! – of the beginning of the performance.
- investigate, explore and find out about sound and music.
  Searching for a particular musical sound quality to create a specific effect is an example common to all composers from infants at a 'sound table' in a corner of the classroom to professional composers **15**

consulting their performing colleagues about the effects obtainable by using various instrumental techniques.

- create something in response to music.
  This area includes responding through another art form such as a sculpture, a poem, a drawing or design. It allows an aesthetic reaction directly in another medium, without the need to translate the effects of music into words.

- use background research and information to understand what they hear in music.
  Knowing a structural convention such as verse-and-chorus or rondo form may heighten understanding of music cast in one of these ways.

- move to music.
  Music and movement both happen within a time continuum and must be internalized within time. Examples here include moving to express oneself, moving to trace the shape or structure of a piece of music, moving to demonstrate awareness of a musical phenomenon – raising a hand when a trill is heard.

- try to achieve an idea which they have already conceived.
  In composing for instance, pupils may first develop an idea in their mind of what effect they are trying to achieve. They may discard several attempts at creating that effect before finally accepting one which matches their intentions.

- choose, select, reject sounds or music.
  Every time we make a choice about what to listen to, from the music of advertisements on television to selecting a recording from a collection, we are appraising.

- use prior experience to understand music.
  Having experienced a particular dance by learning its steps, other musical examples of the same dance may be recognized without further explanation.

- respond verbally to music in questions, opinions, explanations, statements and descriptions.
  This matches the requirements within the revised curriculum to develop a musical vocabulary which is then available for the further development of musical thinking.

Although 'appraising' was an unfamiliar term when the 1992 curriculum was published, it was not fully defined there. The relevant Attainment Target then was simply described as

> the development of the ability to listen to and appraise music including knowledge of musical history, our diverse musical culture and a variety of other musical traditions.

Appraising through moving to music — in a circle game

The revised curriculum of 1995 summarizes appraising in the Programme of Study as

> listen to, and develop understanding of, music from different times and places, applying knowledge to their own work; respond to, and evaluate, live performances and recorded music, including their own and others' compositions and performances.

In the more expansive context of this book there is space to include the fuller definition arrived at by the Research Fellow and the team of teachers attached to the RAMP Unit's project.

- Appraising music is an activity which is carried out by pupils in their composing, performing and listening.
- It happens when they:
  listen purposefully to music
  respond thoughtfully to music
  think actively about music
  make choices and evaluative judgements about music
  use an accumulated experience and knowledge to do this.
- It is a way of coming to know and understand the processes involved in music and musical thinking.

This proves to be wholly in accord with the implied aims and stated objectives of the current curriculum.

Appraising compositions while creating and performing them

Common ground

Although, for the purposes of devising a curriculum, the three main activities through which music can be experienced are considered separately, they need to be taught in an integrated and holistic way. So, for example:

- pupils will often **perform** their own **compositions**, singly or in groups
- **improvising** consists of the spontaneous **performing** of music while **composing** it
- pupils will engage in **appraising** their own and each other's **compositions** while creating and **performing** them
- **composing** stimulates a desire to **listen to** and **appraise** the music of established composers to discover how they may have responded to problems.

As mentioned in chapter 1, the revised Order (1995) begins with an exhortation to 'bring together requirements from both Performing and Composing, and Listening and Appraising wherever possible'. It is particularly important that the necessary distinctions between activities, the different words used to define the parts of the curriculum and (in the context of End of Key Stage Descriptions) the Attainment Targets, should not lead to the compartmentalisation of teaching and learning.

Listening

'Listening' implies a conscious awareness that is not necessarily synonymous with 'hearing'. We **hear** all the sounds within earshot but we do not take them all in: we are selective in which ones we choose to **listen** to. The ability to listen is the primary skill in all musical activity. Listening is essential in performing to achieve accuracy of, among other things, pitch, tempo and ensemble playing; whilst in composing, we have to listen, either to actual sounds or imagined ones, to make judgements about particular effects. An important third aspect is listening to live or recorded performances, sometimes called 'listening in audience'. This aspect in turn carries with it notions of recognition, discrimination, critical response and evaluation.

The use of the word 'listening' in the programme area of Listening and Appraising in the (English) National Curriculum refers not only to the limited area of pupils listening to the music of others. The inclusion of the words 'applying knowledge to their own work', makes clear the importance of accurate and perceptive listening in the other activities of Performing and Composing.

Active Attainment Targets

Both the English and the Welsh curricula use present participles, '-ing', to define the musical activities in the body of the curriculum and in the Attainment Targets. This reflects the importance of the **process** of engaging in musical activities as well as the **product** – the music itself and the musical understanding – which may result from them. In the teaching and learning of music, the process may at times be more significant than its product.

This is also relevant to assessment. The quality of a concert performance, a finished composition, or a conclusive expression of opinion about a piece of music which has just been heard, does not in itself necessarily signal success or failure in the attempt to engage in the activity. The quality and sophistication of decision-making will develop with age and experience and be one of the principal ways in which **progression** will be measured in pupils working within the music curriculum.

This is dealt with further in chapter 6.

Musical elements: general

The music curriculum, both for England and for Wales, provides in the Programmes of Study a list of musical 'elements'. The expectations spelled out in each Key Stage clearly suggest progression throughout the **19** age-range for which the curriculum is designed. (Although specific quotation is from the English curriculum, the principles apply equally to the curriculum for Wales.) So:

- at Key Stage 1, pupils should be 'recognising the musical elements'
- at Key Stage 2, pupils should be 'distinguishing the musical elements'
- at Key Stage 3, pupils should be 'discriminating within and between the musical elements'.

Similarly, the scope of each element expands to indicate progression from one Key Stage to the next, as becomes clear in the following table.

Element	Key Stage 1	Key Stage 2	Key Stage 3
Pitch	High/low	Gradations of pitch	Various scales and modes
Duration	Long/short; pulse or beat; rhythm	Groups of beats; rhythm	Syncopation; rhythm
Dynamics	Loud/quiet/ silence	Different levels of volume; accent	Subtle differences in volume
Tempo	Fast/slow	Different speeds	Subtle differences in speed
Timbre	Quality of sound	Different qualities	Different ways timbre is changed; different qualities
Texture	Several sounds played or sung at the same time/one sound on its own	Different ways sounds are put together	Density and transparency of instrumentation; polyphony; harmony
The use of the above within **structure**	Different sections; repetition	Different ways sounds are organized in simple forms	Forms based on single ideas; forms based on alternating ideas; forms based on developmental ideas

In the 1992 Order the elements were listed for only the Listening and Appraising Attainment Target (called simply Appraising in the Welsh curriculum). The placing of the elements, in the new (1995) Order, among the requirements common to the **whole** curriculum is a thoroughly welcome improvement, as they are equally important as guides to analysing and decision-making about music in the other two activities of Performing and Composing. Pupils should not on any account be led to assume that the elements are simply tools of musical analysis to be used merely in relation to other people's performances and compositions. They should be also using them constantly in making judgements about their **own** music-making.

Expressive and structural elements

Pupils often find it a great deal easier to create expressive sound than to organize it in structures. So it may be helpful to create a division between aspects of the elements which are primarily used as a means of musical **expression** and those which are used primarily to create musical **structures**. Although such a division is rather arbitrary, it may serve as a means of reminding pupils about the need to structure their music, and give teachers a simple check-list for suggesting ways of doing so.

Expressive aspects

- **Pitch**, melody, harmony.
- **Duration**, rhythm.
- **Dynamics**, silence.
- **Tempo**, speed.
- **Timbre**.
- **Texture**, articulation.

These elements normally manifest emotions, feelings and ideas. Again, their use is not exclusively expressive. The way in which they are ordered may also contribute to the structure of music. So, while the contrasting timbres of a single singer and a choir of voices may have an **expressive** effect, they may also create a **structure** – of verse/chorus perhaps.

Structural aspects

- **Pitch**, interval, motif, phrase, chord, cadence.
- **Duration**, pulse.
- **Structure**, form.

21

These elements are normally arranged and inter-related in the creating of a musical composition. Their use, though, is not exclusively structural. They may also contribute to the expression of emotions, feelings and ideas in music. So, while a four-bar phrase may balance a previous one **structurally**, it could also create **expressive** tension, perhaps by being longer, or louder, or higher or faster ...

Form, structure and characteristics

The Music Working Group was also concerned to clarify three other words and their musical associations. All three of these remain in the revised Order (1995).

Form was used to imply a pre-determined mould within which music is constructed. So a composer may plan to write music in ternary form or in a form alternating verse and chorus.

Structure was used to refer to how a composer chooses to arrange and inter-relate the music of a composition, often within a form. So, within the conventional form of a minuet and trio, the decisions a composer may make about, say, the number and length of phrases are **structural**.

Finally, the term **characteristics** was coined to describe the distinctive qualities in any piece of music which arise from the interaction of the elements from which it is made. So, the four-square metre and the timbres of drums and brass instruments may contribute towards the characteristics of a march, while those of a lullaby may arise from a quietly sung melody in a lilting triple time.

It is, of course, essential to understand the meaning and implications of the words performing, composing, (listening) and appraising. But they become effective only when presented to pupils in a planned and structured way – the subject of chapter 3.

3 Planning for music in the classroom

John Stephens, David Adams, Kevin Adams, Michael Brewer, Linda Read

---

Planning is the key to effective learning. It is an essential initial stage for the process of teaching and learning.

Planning for the delivery of the music curriculum in a school requires both formal and informal debate and discussion amongst the teachers. There are five stages in the planning process:

1 **Aims and objectives** – what are we required to teach?
2 **Resources** – what have we got to deliver the curriculum?
3 **Development** – what further resources are required?
4 **Delivery** – how are we to organize the learning and resources?
5 **Evaluation** – have we achieved our objectives?

Aims and objectives

The aims of the music curriculum must relate to the overall aims which a school has set for itself. They will therefore embrace social and spiritual aspects in addition to straightforward musical matters.

The objectives are the specific skills, knowledge and understanding within the field of music which pupils are to be taught.

Broad aims and objectives are set out in chapter 1. These relate to the requirements of the National Curriculum. In many schools these requirements will be regarded as the core of studies to which distinctive and enriching aspects of musical understanding will be added. In various forms the aims and objectives may be used by a school to inform parents and prospective parents and governors, as well as members of the teaching staff, visitors and OFSTED inspectors.

> **Scenario**
> The three teachers in a village primary school met at the end of another busy teaching day to consider another 'official' document entitled '*Music in the National Curriculum – draft proposals*'. They had already worked their way through seven other documents with different subject titles, so they had sorted out a method of operating.

They took it in turn to write out their discussion and shape it into a curriculum statement. 'We want all of our pupils to enjoy music,' they began. 'Of course, enjoyment cannot be guaranteed,' remarked the Head. 'We must ensure that all pupils have the necessary skills.'
'And whose music must they enjoy?' queried the youngest of the three. A few weeks later the next section of the school handbook was completed...

Music

We aim to make music enjoyable for all pupils in the school. They sing, play instruments and listen to music, and will have opportunities to make their own musical compositions. There are regular weekly music lessons and many informal opportunities, both in and out of school, for music-making.

Music is used in the daily assembly and in dance and movement lessons. The school has a good range of percussion instruments which the pupils learn to play to accompany their songs and to make up their own pieces. They are encouraged to listen attentively and use musical words to talk about the music they listen to and make up and perform themselves.

Music-making is an important part of the social and community life of our school.

Resources

At a review or audit of the resources a school has to achieve, the stated aims and objectives should include the following.

1 **Teachers** – the skills, knowledge and experience of the teaching staff, including visiting instrumental tutors and support staff.
2 **Time** – the time allocated for music making activities.
3 **Space** – the spaces used for music activities including, where appropriate, the storage of instruments.
4 **Equipment** – the materials used in music lessons, including song books, scores, tapes and CDs; musical instruments, audio equipment and, where appropriate, computers.
5 **Pupils** – the experience and skill pupils bring to the lessons.

In reviewing resources it will be important to define what, in the professional judgement of the staff, is required to deliver the curriculum. The review will take account of what the school has, and define what needs to be developed.

Scenario

The Head of Music in a large inner-city comprehensive school has been asked by her Head to review the resources for music in the school prior to an expected OFSTED inspection. She plans to draw up a list to present to the members of her department, which consists of one part-time colleague and five visiting instrumental teachers.

She lists the number of professional development courses undertaken by the staff, and notes that they have done relatively little in the way of developing their knowledge and skills in music from other traditions and cultures.

She lists the time allocation for music lessons for each year and notes that, once again, Year 9 receives less time than Years 7 and 8.

The school is well provided for in accommodation for music activities: there are practice rooms, storage and two large teaching rooms. The school was built for more pupils than it now contains!

Although the range of instruments and equipment provides for the current needs, the Head of Department knows that quite a lot of the stock is coming to the end of its serviceable life. She begins to list an order of priority to replace and update the audio equipment, electronic instruments and computer hardware, and for the maintenance of pianos and other instruments. Knowing that the school will not be able to budget for all these items in one school year, she groups them into five categories, one for each of the next five years.

She presents this list to the Head and governors as another contribution to the school's Development Plan.

Development

The Development Plan, or Action Plan as it is sometimes called, identifies the areas where the school wishes to establish or extend its range of resources. For example, a programme to enhance and improve the skills of the staff will be incorporated into this plan, alongside additions and replacement of equipment, and enhancement of the teaching materials.

Delivery

The delivery of the curriculum will include a scheme which defines the opportunities pupils have to develop skills, knowledge and understanding. In many schools the scheme of work is based on units or modules covering a half term's work.

Scenario

The music Co-ordinator in a primary school is preparing the details of plans for the coming half-term. She has mapped out six 'lessons' for each year group, based on the topic or theme that the class teachers have told her they will be following.

She ensures that each lesson includes some singing, and that pupils will be given opportunities to make up music of their own and listen to music performed by other pupils.

The six lessons take account of the stage of musical experience of each class, and give an indication of how the tasks may be differentiated to suit all the pupils including those who are having instrumental lessons and the special needs pupils in each class.

When she has completed these outline plans, she checks each year group for progression, breadth, balance, relevance and continuity.

Her next task will be to present the plan to the teachers at the next staff meeting.

Evaluation

Any scheme of work should include within it a specified time at which the scheme will be reviewed and its effectiveness evaluated.

Programmes of Study

The Programmes of Study provide the framework for planning the curriculum in schools. They are the basis which teachers can use in preparing schemes of work and planning the essential experiences for their pupils' musical development.

Reactions to the new format of the Programmes of Study suggest that the process of planning has been made easier. With the primacy of the Programmes of Study it is hoped that schools will move away from using the End of Key Stage Statements, as they were called, as a basis for planning and focus on the holistic planning of the curriculum.

The Programmes of Study contain fields of musical activity (Performing and Composing, Listening and Appraising for schools in England and Performing, Composing and Appraising in Wales), and the delivery of the curriculum is expected to relate these.

Some general considerations

Formal and informal consultations about planning should involve all teachers who are responsible for pupils' musical development, including instrumental tutors and, on occasions, professional musicians who may from time to time work on projects in a school.

Inevitably initial discussions will centre around the content of lessons. Which songs will be sung? Which pieces of music will be listened to? Such discussions will be valuable if they lead to general considerations of broader issues. A vocabulary, some might say jargon, has grown up around the notion of planning and these terms include:

- **Progression** – are the pupils developing skills and understanding; is their knowledge of music increasing; and most importantly, is the quality of their work improving?
- **Breadth** – the range of musical experience, incorporating music which would otherwise be outside the pupils' experience.
- **Balance** – incorporating activities of composing, performing, listening and appraising, vocal and instrumental.
- **Relevance** – using material which is appropriate to the age, interests and levels of ability of pupils.
- **Continuity** – building upon previous experience.
- **Differentiation** – ensuring that pupils are treated as individuals, recognising that each develops at their own pace, has their own range of skills and understanding, and unique interests and motivation.

Schemes of work

Through the detailed schemes of work developed by teachers, pupils should experience a variety of tasks designed to develop their competence and confidence. For younger pupils, singing, playing simple instruments, exploring and experimenting with sound, listening and composing will often be integrated into a broad scheme of activities and closely related to other aspects of learning. For older pupils, as specific musical interests and skills develop, the detailed schemes of work should seek to encourage progression related to those interests and skills, whilst continuing to provide an integrated experience of the three main areas of activity.

Throughout the curriculum, progression can be viewed in three dimensions:

1 **Range** – the increasing variety of instruments, musical forms, repertoire encountered by pupils.
2 **Demand** – the length of a composition, the level of instrumental or vocal skill, the complexity of repertoire required of pupils.
3 **Quality** – the integrity and originality of a composition, the expressive level of performance, the perceptions and reasoning applied to music heard by pupils.

For older pupils, specific musical interests and skills develop...

Scenario

Two Year 7 pupils have been set a task to improvise over a 12-bar Blues sequence during a music lesson. They share an electronic keyboard.

'Didn't you do this sort of thing in your primary school?' asks one boy.

'Yes, but we didn't have electronic instuments. We only used xylophones which we had to take the notes off if they weren't needed,' replies his partner.

They practise the chord sequence with one player operating the keyboard whilst his partner checks the notes. They write out the sequence and then begin work on the improvisation.

'I think this sounds better.'

'Well, let's try it again.'

'We could make it long – and I think it should start quiet and end up very loud.'

The finished composition is played to the class during the next lesson, after the two pupils, and their classmates who have been given the same task, have had more time to refine their pieces.

Although the means of organizing and presenting learning tasks and material will change as pupils mature, much of the content will be repeated and covered in different, often more complex ways in each Key Stage. As with most other subjects, there will be a continuous process of consolidating and developing skills and knowledge previously introduced.

In its final report (1991), the Music Working Group suggested general provisions which should apply at all Key Stages, as well as detailed provisions applying at each particular stage. This principle has been restored in the revised Order (1995).

The format of the new Orders will assist planning. The English Order does this by laying out in six numbered paragraphs the Programme of Study for each Key Stage. Paragraphs 1, 2 and 3 trace progression through each Key Stage; for example, paragraph 1b progresses thus:

Key Stage 1 – 'use of IT to record sounds'
Key Stage 2 – 'use of IT to explore and record sounds'
Key Stage 3 – 'use of IT to explore, create and record sounds'.

Paragraph 2a expands the concept of pitch as follows:

Key Stage 1 – 'high/low'
Key Stage 2 – 'gradations of pitch'
Key Stage 3 – 'various scales and modes'.

In paragraph 3, the repertoire chosen for performing and listening expands from two simple categories at Key Stage 1 to five categories at Key Stage 3.

The fourth paragraph, however, is common to all three Key Stages. **Pupils should be given** [the same] **opportunities** for performing and composing, listening and appraising, from the ages of five to fourteen. They are to be re-visited many times, and of course the specific skills and knowledge gained at one Key Stage will be taken into account, reinforced and developed at subsequent Key Stages.

This heading contains six sub-sections, as follows.

Pupils should be given opportunities to:

a   control sounds made by the voice and a range of tuned and untuned instruments

b   perform with others, and develop awareness of audience, venue and occasion

c   compose in response to a variety of stimuli, and explore a range of resources, *e.g. voices, instruments, sounds from the environment*

d   communicate musical ideas to others

e   listen to, and develop understanding of, music from different times and places, applying knowledge to their own work

f   respond to, and evaluate, live performances and recorded music, including their own and others' compositions and performances.

As we noted in chapter 1, the weighting which was omitted from the 1992 Order is now present by implication; two of these 'opportunities' refer to performing, two to composing and two to listening and appraising.

(The curriculum for Wales is laid out rather differently, but the same principles apply.)

Scenario

The Governor looked at the candidate who had answered fluently all the questions posed by other members of the interviewing panel. He asked:

'And what will you expect the pupils to be able to do, and know about music at the end of a school year, which they could not do and did not know at the beginning?'

There was a pause.

'Well,' said the candidate. 'I will want them to develop the skills and sensitivities of using their ear more acutely. They'll perform with greater confidence and accuracy on instruments, and with their voices. I'd want them to be able to make up their own pieces and gain enjoyment and satisfaction from this, and I'd expect them to listen with greater understanding, and be able to talk about the music they hear.'

'And what about pupils who are tone deaf, like me?' quizzed the Governor.

'I believe anyone who can hear has all that's required to be musical,' responded the candidate, who then thought that, for the benefit of the Head, he had better qualify this statement.

'Pupils grow at different rates, and in music they develop at different speeds. They are often motivated by particular interests. So in class lessons I try to make sure that there are opportunities for pupils to get a sense of achievement in various ways, exploiting and developing their particular skills and talents. This sometimes means giving them different tasks to do, or sometimes accepting different results. I'm always expecting the best – in my classes I believe and expect that pupils will work well.'

The interview ended. It seemed an age before the Chair of Governors was congratulating the successful candidate.

Careful planning will be needed, both to provide for progression, and to cater for the needs of pupils of a wide range of ability. A range of opportunities will provide for individual needs by either setting different tasks or expecting different outcomes. As an aid to that planning, teachers will have available various forms of support, including radio and television broadcasts, published material, programmes for professional development, and in many areas the expertise of visiting instrumental teachers and other professional musicians. Activities and tasks may be initiated by pupils as well as teachers and, particularly in the case of older pupils, they should be designed to encourage independent study. They should also relate, so far as practicable, to the range of provision for musical activity outside the classroom.

The categories of teaching strategies, content, processes and skills provide a framework for developing a scheme. In simple terms this means:

- how the learning will be organized – **teaching strategies**
- what material will be used – **content**
- understanding the learning and experiencing the activity – **process**
- reaching specific competencies or fulfilling a task – **skills**.

Teachers often make these distinctions to assist their planning. It is also important to recognize that, in some musical activities, the process features more prominently than the product, whilst at times the product provides a focus. The means of securing both will be determined by the range and effectiveness of teaching strategies.

Teaching strategies

The musical achievements of pupils, and their motivation to engage in activities in music lessons, are significantly influenced by the strategies teachers adopt in the classroom. There will be occasions when the teacher directs and leads. There will be others when his or her role should focus upon encouraging, giving advice and facilitating – as, for example, when pupils are developing their own ideas in musical composition. The most effective strategy will be that which is best suited to the task or activity being undertaken.

Effective strategies will also relate to the levels of maturity, skills and experience of the pupils. They will be designed to give pupils progressively more responsibility for planning, presenting and evaluating; and will guide them to the point where they can express independent preferences based on a broad experience and understanding of the subject.

Scenario

The student-teacher and her supervisor were discussing a series of lessons which she had prepared for a forthcoming teaching practice in a local primary school. The student had prepared material for the lesson – some songs and activities.

The supervisor asked how the pupils would be organized for the proposed activity.

'I prefer to let them work in friendship groups – it seems to get the best results.'

'Have you tried any other means of grouping? How can you assess that your system is the most effective?'

Thus began a discussion on ways of grouping pupils for specific activities. Together, they considered friendship groups, random groups, ability groups, interest groups, pupils who play the same instrument ... and this developed further into a discussion about group size.

The student realized that, as well as content and material, she needed to consider how the pupils might be organized to achieve the most effective outcomes.

The theory became stark reality when her teaching practice began.

Content

The choice and selection of material for music activities will vary from school to school, and will be developed on the range of existing materials and the confidence and skill of teachers to use them. One of the functions of a music co-ordinator in a primary school is to ensure that the teaching staff have access to suitable songs, instrumental pieces and music for listening and a range of instruments appropriate to the age groups within the school.

One aspect of the content of the music curriculum which exercised the Music Working Group, and is still of crucial importance, is the relationship between **knowledge** and **understanding**. At various stages during the transformation of the Group's final report (1991) to the statutory National Curriculum in Music, it sensed a desire in some quarters to introduce the requirement of factual knowledge for its own sake. The inclusion in the 1992 Orders of the words 'including knowledge of musical history' was resented by many teachers for appearing to invite the study of factual knowledge unrelated to direct musical experience. The revised (1995) Orders clearly require the integration of knowledge with the experiencing of music aurally. Five fields of knowledge which pupils require are newly and explicitly defined as follows. (Specific references are to the English format but, as elsewhere, the same principles apply within the curriculum for Wales.)

1 Knowledge of the musical elements (listed and defined in paragraph 2, one of the three paragraphs which relate to all work within the Programmes of Study).

2 Knowledge of musical resources – the instruments available for which to compose; what they can be made to do – the technological potential of an electronic keyboard or the timbral qualities of which tabla or violin are capable; and the role of the people involved in playing them (detailed in paragraph 6a, across all Key Stages in the field of Listening and Appraising).

3 Knowledge of how music is communicated – how the knowledge in 1 and 2 above inter-relates to create means of communication. If the elements and the instrumental and human resources are seen as the 'effectors' of musical communication, they combine and relate together to produce 'effects'. (Paragraph 6b across the three Key Stages cover and exemplify this field of knowledge.)

4 Knowledge of how music reflects its historical and social context, and how these contexts influence music (detailed in paragraph 6c).

5 Knowledge of musical character, styles and traditions – especially how music changes or stays the same across different times and places. This puts spontaneous, 'one-off' musical experience into its broader musical context, identifying what, in a piece of music, is unique and what is common ground.

Above all it is essential that knowledge is developed through experience rather than by didactic instruction, and that it is largely derived from, and applied to, pupils' own work within the music curriculum. In fact, paragraph 4e in the revised Order places emphasis on this approach: 'applying knowledge to their own work'.

A large range of specific suggestions for content are to be found in the list of publications in chapter 7.

Process

Pupils' motivation, and therefore their capacity to learn, is enhanced by activities which are challenging, enjoyable and recognized by them as relevant and attainable. They are also stimulated by opportunities to take responsibility for their own learning. The processes suggested in the Programmes of Study for music are designed to ensure that activities of these kinds are encouraged, and that pupils can be offered the experience and practice needed to acquire the necessary skills.

There are key words in the revised Programmes of Study which imply the process of development through an engagement in the activities of music. Thus, in composing, 'explore, create, select and organize sounds in simple structures' at Key Stage 1 proceeds to 'explore, create, select, combine and organize sounds in musical structures' at Key Stage 2 and then to 'select and combine resources and develop musical ideas within musical structures' at Key Stage 3.

Skills

Skills in this context relate to the competencies in listening, composing and performing which pupils acquire through experience and practice, up to the point where they can achieve a given task with confidence and fluency.

Singing

Singing (which encompasses improvisation with vocal sounds) is a requirement in the Programme of Study at all Key Stages. If developed consistently, singing provides a central resource in performing and composing at every level. It will, for most pupils, strengthen the acquisition of aural perception and aural memory, which may lead naturally to the learning of written notation.

Provided the voice is not strained at any level through use of extremes of dynamics or pitch, it can be used musically and expressively right through adolescence. However, it is very important that young voices are nurtured while they are involved in musical activities. Since the physical apparatus of the voice does not finally settle until well after

Singing — a central resource at every level

school age, it is essential that voices are used sensitively. The following are some pointers to good practice:

1   If the vocal chords are not energized by breath they are put under considerable strain. Basic breathing exercises are not only helpful but vital before singing takes place. They are also very simple, and can be absorbed after only a few repetitions. Any exercise which involves full inhalation and exhalation, awareness of the rib cage and the function of the diaphragm and abdominal muscles will enable young singers to experience the sensation of supporting the sound which they make, and to gain immediate control over the sound-making process.

2   The repertoire chosen for singing should be progressive in its demands upon the voice, particularly in terms of pitch range. At Key Stage 1 it is best to concentrate on tunes of limited range and to avoid repertoire with wide leaps. In Key Stage 2, both the lower and upper ranges can be extended gently, but care should be taken to place songs so that their greater part lies in the centre of the voice. Much repertoire now being used in schools concentrates on the lower end of pupils' vocal range. Sounds in the upper register – the 'head voice' – are easy to achieve, and again simple exercises will assist, which can be in the form of games. Simple folk songs from many countries are ideal in combining a limited pitch range with repetition of patterns.

The voice – an important ingredient in all aspects of music making

3   Where singers choose to use the so-called 'belting' style (in which the voice is sometimes pushed to produce loud sounds without breath support), the use of microphones will enable them to achieve an appropriate balance with accompanying instruments without subjecting the voice to the risks of strain.

4   The process of 'warming up' is essential when anybody sings. This can be achieved through a gradually widening range of dynamics and pitch, and can come from the repertoire which is being sung.

5   The voice is an important ingredient in all aspects of music making, not only in singing songs. It is available for use in creating harmony, in improvisation, and in every kind of musicianship training – sight-reading, identifying intervals, and so on. The richness and variety of vocal timbre arises from the ability of the voice to make the whole range of vowel sounds. This can be achieved by singing songs in different languages, by playing games using different vowel sounds, from the earliest stages of school life. Such music-making can integrate naturally with drama and word-games.

6   Teachers should take care of their own voices too. In rehearsal, and even in controlling a class, signs and non-verbal instructions can reduce the strain on this most precious instrument.

Notation

36   The word 'notation' is used to refer to any means of expressing the

elements of music in written form. Young pupils acquire an awareness of musical elements (for example, high and low, quiet and loud, long and short) through repeated sound-making and listening. In the early stages, teachers may use a three-dimensional object or objects to represent a sound or a pattern of sounds. This can lead to the use of graphic notation, in which elements such as exact pitch may not be precisely identified. Similarly, the density of a texture can be indicated by the thickness of a line, and differences in timbre by the use of different colours.

Through such improvisation and discovery, pupils can come to recognize the need to notate the music they are making, and attempt to meet that need. Awareness of relative pitch may be reinforced by the use of hand signs (such as those used according to the principles of Curwen or Kodály), and these in turn may lead to the use of letter names for pitches (some teachers use sol-fa), or a numbering system. Notational systems, including staff notation, can thus be approached through active music-making. The English curriculum requires notations to be introduced to all pupils during Key Stage 2, and specifies conventional staff notation, where appropriate, in Key Stage 3. The Welsh curriculum requires appropriate notations in Key Stage 3. It should be borne in mind that pupils generally acquire facility in performing from notation before they develop the skill and understanding needed to notate their own and others' compositions.

In some traditions, musical ideas are communicated aurally. In others,

Staff notation — at Key Stage 3

a variety of forms of notation are used, and these should be taught where appropriate. Chord symbols, for example, are used in a wide range of musical traditions, including much pop and jazz music. The function of notation will only be fully understood if it is taught in the context of practical music-making and is seen as a relevant skill. The learning of notation divorced from sound can be said to negate its function and to be arid study unrelated to music itself.

Conclusion

Planning is part of a process which begins with defining the aims, continues through clarifying the objectives, planning how to achieve them, delivering them to the classes, and ends with evaluating whether or not the intended learning has actually taken place.

However daunting the initial task of planning may appear, once begun, subsequent development becomes a logical part of this sequence.

As such, it is not a fixed tablet to be left, once concluded, but a continuing process which needs to be kept constantly under review.

4 Equal opportunities in music

George Pratt

All pupils, regardless of social, ethnic and cultural origins, gender, and physical and mental ability, have the right to experience, enjoy and express themselves in music. In fact, music can often have a special role to play in breaking down barriers between pupils and releasing their creative potential.

In order to open up opportunities for all, we need to bear three points in mind.

1 **Pupils** may need positive steering towards musical activities and experiences in which they can succeed.
2 The actual **tasks** towards which we steer pupils may need to be adapted so that they can respond to them.
3 Additional **resources** may be needed if we are to ensure that all pupils really are offered equal opportunities.

These points apply to many pupils with no obvious disability. For example, there are innumerable people who, because as children they had not yet mastered the connection between ears and larynx, between hearing sounds and making them, were scorned as 'groaners', told not to take part in singing, and remain tragically convinced even as adults that they are 'unmusical'. How different things might have been if someone had steered them towards making a contribution in a different way, perhaps by clapping the pulse as a rhythmic accompaniment (1 above), or if the pitch and range of music had been adapted to suit their developing voices (2 above), or if an instrument had been available for them to play alongside the singers (3, providing a resource).

There are, though, four areas which do require some special care.

1 Cultural heritage and diversity

Music provides exceptional opportunities for all of us to experience the cultural heritages of other people, from within the United Kingdom, from other countries and from different religious and ethnic origins. As we have made clear in chapter 2, this rich variety of cultural heritage can, and should, be reflected in the repertoire for teaching and learning **39** music. If a school is fortunate enough to have pupils from a variety of cultural backgrounds, there will be opportunities for sharing their contrasting experiences through musical activities – singing each others' songs, playing each others' instruments, learning about festivals or other occasions for which various kinds of music is intended. Such sharing from the inside, rather than merely observing from the outside, as a curiosity, can not only bring pupils into contact with a fascinating range of musical experiences but can lead to music being a positive force for cultural tolerance.

Musical skills and understanding will be enhanced if pupils are introduced to specific examples of music from different cultures and styles. Although pupils can be introduced to music from other cultures by recognising elements which it has in common with music which is more familiar to them, different kinds of music should so far as possible retain their cultural and stylistic identity. By the time, say, an eastern European folk song has been translated and accompanied by untypical harmonies on a piano, it may have lost a lot of its true character. There will, though, be times when a meeting of contrasting cultures may provide a legitimate musical fusion – of styles, of instrumental tone colours, and of verbal language both sung to existing music and set to music newly-composed.

Several practical issues arise.

- Language can be problematic for pupils whose mother tongue is not English – or in Welsh-medium schools, for those whose mother tongue is not Welsh. This is particularly true in the early primary years. Problems can be minimized by taking particular care that terminology is clear and understood – and by avoiding technical language as far as possible. Music lessons can in fact provide valuable opportunities for language learning, through practical experience in songs and singing games, through collaborative activities between pupils with different mother tongues and through pupils' desire to express and to appraise, in words, what they have experienced in music.
- Some activities, particularly those involving dance and pop music, may raise concerns or even be quite unacceptable among parents from particular religions and cultural groups. It may be necessary to discuss issues like these sympathetically, with both parents and pupils, and even to modify some of the activities to avoid offending religious and cultural sensitivities.
- Some cultures, and some individual parents within them, introduce children more readily than others to singing at the pre-school age. Children who have not listened to singing and have not sung themselves, as a matter of course, are likely to be less developed vocally

than others. All too easily this can be interpreted as having 'a poor ear', when in fact it is no more than a later development of the link between hearing sounds and reproducing them with the voice.

■ Teachers may hesitate to introduce particular musical traditions because they lack the authentic equipment for them. Rather than omitting such traditions from pupils' experience, it is better to improvise. For example, African rhythms can be performed on available western instruments; remarkable examples exist of gamelans made from scrap metal; Regional Arts Boards have funded the employment of people with the skill to tune a set of oil drums as the basis of an Afro-Caribbean steel band.

■ Relations and friends of pupils may be willing to bring into the school their particular enthusiasms, skills, instruments and recordings of all traditions to share with the pupils.

■ Many LEAs have managed still to retain their music support services. Others have delegated them to charitable trusts. From all of these, professional help can be sought, sometimes for a fee, sometimes free of charge. In many cases, such help can also be sought from schemes run by bodies like the Regional Arts Boards, Education Officers appointed to symphony orchestras, Community Arts organisations, Afro-Caribbean and South Asian music and dance and theatre groups. Teachers cannot be expected to have mastery of all styles and cultures, but they can widen pupils' experiences through imaginative organisation of whatever help and stimulus may be available.

The Muslim Educational Trust, 130 Stroud Green Road, London N4 3RZ, has produced a short pamphlet entitled 'Muslims, music and the National Curriculum' which provides a helpful perspective for teachers seeking to reconcile the requirements of the National Curriculum and the wishes and religious beliefs of the Muslim community.

2 Sex and gender

There is only one respect in which pupils' musical activities need be influenced by their sex. It is with the changing voice at puberty, more disturbing to some boys than to girls, though to some extent common to both. The National Curriculum has retained through all Key Stages the requirement to sing as well as to play. But it recognizes the need to nurture and protect changing voices by leaving open the option that they may be used only in group performance rather than in a solo capacity. Teachers will need to be particularly careful in choosing the total range and the most comfortable area of pitch demanded of voices at this stage. This issue has been dealt with more fully in chapter 3.

Enquiries during the preparation of the National Curriculum in Music **41** discovered that roughly twice as many girls as boys learn instruments, and the proportions get more out of balance in woodwind and strings. It seems, therefore, that the opening up of a lifetime's enjoyment of music-making may be denied to many boys in particular. To counter this, it may prove advisable to engage in some 'positive discrimination' – for example, by starting boys-only choirs – in the face of what appears to be peer group pressure for boys to conceal their musical sensitivity and potential. On the other hand, micro technology and pop music seem to have attracted more boys to GCSE music courses since they began. Clearly this is a welcome trend – but again it may conceal a disinclination on the part of girls towards these areas of musical experience.

There are other areas in which gender stereotyping may arise in music, and teachers need to guard against them, to ensure that pupils' choices are based on genuine music preferences. At the primary level, for example, large, loud-sounding instruments (drums, cymbals, mini-basses) should not be only the preserve of boys. At secondary level, teachers might well check that the composers studied and mentioned are not exclusively male.

3   Music for pupils with special educational needs

The range of educational needs is both wide and diverse, extending from mild degrees of learning difficulty to profound and multiple physical and mental disabilities. In a small minority of cases, pupils' patterns of behaviour or inability to share in musical experience and achievement may lead teachers to the conclusion that the challenges of some aspects of the music curriculum may be unsuitable for them and they need either 'temporary exception' or 'disapplication' from the music curriculum. This should be very rare indeed, though – virtually all pupils can follow the music curriculum to some degree.

This view was confirmed by a very wide range of advisers to the Music Working Group, all of whom agreed not only that pupils with special needs should follow the curriculum if at all possible, but also that they should be integrated with other pupils in mainstream primary and secondary schools when doing so.

What may vary, however, is the balance between the three activities – performing, composing and appraising – and among the levels of achievement which can be reached within each of them. But music lends itself particularly well to differentiation by outcomes as well as by task. Most learning in music is linear and cumulative rather than self-contained and finite. Pupils sing and play from the age of five right through to fourteen – and, we hope, beyond. They continue to listen and compose throughout the age range, and to deepen their knowledge and understanding of music. A positive approach for teachers is to look for

abilities rather than the **disabilities** of pupils with special educational needs, and to identify those activities across the Programmes of Study and through the Key Stages which will best allow their pupils to:

- experience a sense of achievement and worth
- develop confidence
- make an identifiable individual contribution
- be sensitive to the musical activities and creation of others.

Of course, **every** pupil has different educational needs. But these differences may well be more evident among pupils with special educational needs, and there are strategies for meeting many of them. Here are some examples.

- **Musical material** may be adapted to meet special needs. For example, pupils with non-verbal communication may well be able to hum, to contribute other body sounds such as a cough or a clap, or to perform on instruments.
- **Instruments** may be adapted or selected to suit pupils with severe physical disabilities. Hand chimes, for instance, may be easier to manage than bars requiring beaters. Instruments which transmit strong vibrations will help those with impaired hearing. The 'Common Requirements' of the 1995 Orders specifically notes the need to provide 'aids or adapted equipment to allow access to practical activities within and beyond school'.
- **Other resources** may need to be adapted or selected – for instance, large print or raised notations for the partially sighted. Again, the 'Common Requirements' refer to non-sighted methods of reading such as Braille, and also to 'non-visual or non-aural ways of acquiring information'.
- Acquiring **computer equipment and software** is recognized in the 'Common Requirements – Access' section as possibly needing a particularly high priority, so that pupils can compose with programs which allow selection, ordering and other manipulations of musical material simply by touching buttons.
- It may be necessary to change **the order of the curriculum** for pupils with muscular dystrophy and progressive diseases of the nervous system, in order to sustain a sense of rewarding experiences for as long as possible as the physical condition deteriorates.

Music therapy, undertaken by a qualified music therapist, can assist in diagnosing and remedial treatment of specific emotional, physical, social and learning disorders.

Details of organisations which can offer advice on providing for special educational needs are listed in the British Music Education Yearbook, **43** published annually by Rhinegold Publishing Ltd, 241 Shaftesbury Avenue, London WC2H 8EJ.

Summary
- Pupils with special educational needs should be encouraged to follow the National Curriculum to the maximum extent possible.
- Differentiation by the levels of outcome, measurable by the End of Key Stage Descriptions, as well as by the nature of tasks, defined by the Programmes of Study should allow almost all pupils with special educational needs to participate in the experiences of all the musical activities – Composing and Performing, Listening and Appraising.
- Teachers should think out and try imaginative and unconventional ways to enable pupils to achieve through their abilities, rather than being frustrated by their disabilities.

4 The needs of the musically very able

Potential talent must not go unrecognized and undeveloped. If it does, it is a loss both to the individual pupil, for whom there could be the reward of a lifetime of great personal satisfaction, and also to society, which depends on such talent for the next generation of professional and amateur musicians to maintain and develop the vitality of our musical cultures.

Pupils who are potentially very able in music need to be identified in time to allow their ability to develop and flourish. In many cases, talented children are identified and encouraged by parents. But a great responsibility remains first with the primary class teachers and later with instrumental teachers and secondary music specialists. This may include not only identifying such pupils but also making special provisions for them. They will very often need to make an early start on instrumental tuition; they will be helped by the sort of flexible timetabling which allows opportunities for instrumental practice within the school day; they may benefit greatly by having additional breadth of experience through, for example, ensemble work and concert visits.

Pupils may give hints of exceptional potential in too many ways for any simple formula to apply. However there are some common pointers which apply in different degrees to individuals, and a combination of some of them may give real evidence of special musical talent.

- The very able pupil is likely to **get it right** first time, perhaps in imitating a musical phrase on voice or instrument.
- Many exceptional musicians have been able to **memorize** music quickly, even after a first hearing.
- Gifted musicians can sometimes **read** notations with exceptional ease.

- Potential performers, in particular, may be very **well co-ordinated** and show an instinctive rhythmic response, perhaps by dancing or moving in time to a musical pulse.
- A very acute sense of pitch may be shown by **singing** well in tune.
- A few adult musicians have **perfect pitch**, the ability to recall pitch exactly, to sing a particular song always in the same key, to be disturbed when a familiar piece is presented at the wrong pitch. Research suggests that this may be quite common in young children and it may even be destroyed by the presentation of music at a variety of pitches.
- An ability which is difficult to define but easy to identify is the possession of a spontaneous and authentic **creative impulse** in performing and composing. This may show itself in clear initiative in improvisation, perhaps coupled with the desire to take a prominent role or to lead, but equally it may be shown in the pupil who lacks social skills and tends to work alone.
- Potentially gifted pupils may show an **unusual affinity** to a particular instrument, perhaps being unwilling to be parted from it, or responding particularly enthusiastically to it. Often they will be seen to have a particular ease of physical response to it – 'born with a reed in the mouth' or 'a bow in the hand'.
- Another clue is evidence of particular **sensitivity** to music itself, expressed in the turn of a phrase or the joy in a particular musical tone colour.
- But even among the most able, these kinds of sensitivities may not show themselves at an early age, and many achieve a high musical standard simply through **personality, determination** and **sticking power**.
- **Out of school**, gifted young musicians will often engage in a high level of activity, composing spontaneously, responding to private instrumental tuition, or developing a recognized expertise in a local band or group rehearsing on their own initiative.

If the teacher believes that a pupil has exceptional potential in music, there are many ways to create opportunities for its development. These include the following:

- Seeking advice from colleagues, including visiting instrumental teachers, LEA inspectors and directors of music services.
- Discussing with the pupil and advising on the available opportunities to study voice or a preferred choice of instrument.
- Helping to negotiate the acquisition of a suitable instrument, for example from the LEA.
- Encouraging the pupil to take up the opportunities for instrumental **45**

or vocal tuition which may be available through LEA support services or whatever schemes may have developed to replace them.

■ Involving parents in discussions, and advising on the possible social, financial and organisational implications of pursuing a special path in music.

■ Helping to negotiate extra time for pupils to be taught and to practise.

■ Enabling pupils to take part in ensemble performances at a level which makes appropriately high demands on them.

■ Making enquiries about whether, and how, to apply for a funded place at one of the specialist music schools or junior departments of conservatoires.

There is an increasing variety of agencies and arrangements for instrumental tuition outside schools. These include private teachers (listed by the Incorporated Society of Musicians, 10 Stratford Place, London W1N 9AE); independently-run music centres; LEA music centres; the junior departments of music colleges; holiday music courses, run both privately and by LEAs. Junior departments at music colleges provide opportunities for pupils with identified potential and talent. Their programmes are organized mostly within the colleges on Saturdays during term time. Bursaries and LEA scholarships are available for some pupils. Specialist music schools, where boarding education can allow for concentrated musical study alongside a broad curriculum, also provide for exceptionally able pupils. There are some scholarships to these schools provided through funds from central government.

For most pupils, these considerations will not apply. It is vital, though, that where exceptional potential exists it is recognized and responded to – and this responsibility will often begin with the generalist class teacher in a primary school. If a teacher suspects a pupil may potentially be musically very able, it is essential to seek advice – firmly, though without raising hopes and expectations.

5 Support for the music curriculum

John Stephens, Gillian Moore, Julian Smith

The extended curriculum

John Stephens

Musical activities in schools often provide an important focus for their corporate life, projecting an ethos and image for their values, traditions and standards. In many areas the community is enriched by such activities which can range from small scale performances by a few pupils to musical productions, youth choirs, bands and orchestras.

The skills which pupils have been taught in class provide a foundation for them to make useful contributions to many different activities outside the classroom. Such activities are often referred to as 'extra curricular'; they happen because dedicated teachers organize rehearsals and concerts outside normal teaching hours. Where the activities are part of a school's policy and curriculum intention, the term 'extended curriculum' is more precise and appropriate. Such activities are planned in relation to the whole music programme and there is an obligation upon the teacher to deliver them.

Many schools encourage pupils to participate in such activities, and it is clear that those who do so are likely to gain an increased understanding of music and awareness of its varied contexts. Singing and playing instruments are social activities, and accomplishments to be shared with others; much of the satisfaction in musical achievement – and an important means of developing and building upon it – derives from collaborative efforts in choirs, bands, orchestras and other ensembles.

Many primary and secondary schools organize some additional musical activities outside the framework of the school timetable. These provide opportunities to bring together pupils of different ages and stages of musical development in activities which extend and challenge their skills in ways which are not always possible in class lessons. They make a significant contribution to the development of the musically talented, also catering for the needs of a large number of other pupils. A wide variety of groups may be found, covering a range of musical **47** styles, including girls', boys' and mixed choirs; folk, madrigal and rock groups; orchestras and string orchestras; wind, brass, steel and big bands; and chamber and jazz ensembles. In addition, music teachers often work closely with teachers of other subjects on projects such as the production of musicals or operettas.

Community links

Links with the community also provide opportunities for pupils to relate their music-making to a wider social context. This can happen, for example, when pupils from linked mainstream and special schools work together on a composing and performing project; when pupils perform in a hospital; or when they join with a senior citizen's group for a specific project.

Festivals

Many pupils participate in local or national festivals – either competitive, like the eisteddfodau in Wales, or on a non-competitive basis. A large number of performers participate each year in the National Festival of Music for Youth and the Schools Proms which provide examples, often the envy of other countries, of the range and diversity of music making in schools and a measure of the standards achieved. Sometimes groups undertake foreign tours or exchanges, including concert performances. Participation in all such events enables pupils to meet and work together with others who have similar interests from different schools and communities.

Support

The nature and diversity of music activities in schools has been developed and supported by various structures, each playing a distinctive role. The instrumental teaching service, advisory support for teachers' professional development and the increasing involvement of professional musicians operating in various ways directly with pupils in schools, or on the concert platform or opera stage, all contribute to the learning enterprise for which schools have a legal responsibility.

These patterns have emerged, often through inspired pioneers, within the framework of local education authorities. However, the changing structures for funding schools, which place greater responsibility for budgeting and curriculum planning with individual institutions, are in many areas placing a strain upon the broader, authority-wide services which can, at best, take a wider strategic view. It is perhaps most visible in the provision for instrumental music teaching and the orchestras, bands and ensembles which bring together talented pupils from different schools to provide challenges for which individual schools are often not able to cater.

As the pattern of support in this area changes, agencies and trusts are assuming many of the functions previously undertaken by LEAs. Income is necessary to sustain this operation and increasingly parental contributions are required. Not all parents are in a position to make such a contribution, and this places 'at risk' many talented pupils, particularly the 'first generation' musicians in a family. However, money alone is not what is required in this area: structures are needed to ensure opportunities for talented and committed pupils wherever they are from, and in whatever style, culture or genre their talent is manifest, to come together and share their music-making in enterprises which aspire to the highest levels of achievement.

Instrumental music tuition

The underlying aim of the music curriculum is to develop musicianship and understanding through singing, playing, composing and listening. In order that the music curriculum may be delivered comprehensively, and to ensure high standards of achievement, pupils will need to play instruments as well as sing. In the early years, at Key Stage 1, they will use simple instruments such as tuned and untuned percussion instruments, requiring limited technical skills. By Key Stage 2, pupils should be exercising their skills and developing their ideas on a wider range of instruments requiring more sophisticated technical skills. These may be chromatic tuned percussion instruments, recorders, band and orchestral instruments, steel pans, guitar or a keyboard instrument. It will be important for pupils to have experiences which lay secure technical foundations in playing an instrument. The need for specialist instrumental tuition becomes apparent at this stage and continues − for those pupils with the interest and commitment to continue with instrumental study − throughout their schooling. Those who achieve the highest levels of attainment in music have a proficiency as an instrumental performer, with the ability to demonstrate skills in composition by the deployment and use of instruments.

Undertaking the task of developing a skill on a musical instrument requires commitment and application, but there are many transferable skills in the disciplines involved, and the rewards can include lifelong pleasure and satisfaction. For some it will be the start of a vocation. In this respect an early beginning, particularly on stringed instruments, is essential for those who aspire to a career in performance. Opportunities for learning an instrument, the identification of talent, and a coherent **49** music curriculum which is relevant to the principal study of an instrument, are essential to the vocational needs of young musicians.

Specialist tuition

Whilst there is a statutory requirement for all pupils aged five to fourteen in maintained schools to receive a general musical education based on the National Curriculum, there is no statutory obligation that schools offer a range of specialist instrumental tuition.

So of itself, the National Curriculum will not ensure the opportunities for pupils to develop specialist instrumental skills; the range of skills required by amateurs and professionals to reach satisfactory levels of competence on an instrument, or as a composer. A continuum between the general music education and specialist instrumental teaching is required in order to provide opportunities for the development of individual potential. Specialist teachers of instruments make a distinctive contribution to this process.

The Music Working Group was not permitted to include the right to specialist tuition within the National Curriculum, a 'right' that many local education authorities had established within their local rules. The new methods of funding schools, through which instrumental tuition and the provision for group music-making in bands, orchestras and ensembles are no longer provided directly from the local education authority, are placing at risk many of the opportunities built up previously by LEAs. Individual schools are not obliged to co-ordinate or contribute to area or county-wide activities.

These concerns led a group of professional associations, in early 1993, to issue a Statement of Common Purpose.

The associations were:

- Association of British Orchestras
- Committee of Heads of Music Colleges
- Incorporated Society of Musicians
- Music Advisers National Association
- Music Industries Association Education Committee
- Music for Youth
- Schools Music Association
- UK Council for Music Education and Training (now known as the Music Education Council).

This group, with the support from the Arts Council for England and the Calouste Gulbenkian Foundation, commissioned MORI and Coopers & Lybrand to undertake an independent review of instrumental music provision in schools. (Copies of the review can be obtained from the

Incorporated Society of Musicians, 10 Stratford Place, London W1N 9AE.)

Whilst the survey indicated that there was no evidence to suggest a decline in the number of pupils receiving instrumental tuition, it warned of the need for structures to ensure the continuation of area and county groups.

The range of skills and techniques applied to a single instrument is wide, and specialist tuition from an expert is required for high levels of achievement to be reached. Specific techniques are rarely transferable between instruments: flautists have a different range of technique from trumpeters, although both blow into their instruments; kit drummers, tabla players and steel pan players all strike their instruments, but each instrument operates within traditions which have different technical requirements; the violin and the cello are both bowed stringed instruments yet, whilst there are some common features, they are sufficiently differentiated to require specialist teaching. In the acquisition of instrumental skills, therefore, the music curriculum has parallels with the teaching of discrete modern foreign languages: although some relate to each other, all require specialist input.

Specialist teachers, who visit schools to teach pupils specific skills associated with a particular instrument or group of instruments, include those who specialize in keyboard and vocal work, in the more common orchestral and band instruments and, increasingly, in those instruments used in the performance of music from non-European traditions. Many teachers providing instrumental tuition have developed strategies for group and ensemble tuition, and are now closely relating their approaches to those used in class lessons.

Instrumental music services

Recent changes, including the delegation of budgets to schools and the legal position relating to charging parents for instrumental music lessons for groups of up to four pupils, have affected the provision and delivery of instrumental tuition in all parts of the country.

The responsibility for delivering the curriculum is an increasing concern for governors and headteachers. Decisions have to be taken and priorities established. In some areas the support for instrumental tuition in schools is provided by an agency or a service unit of a local authority, or in some cases a trust. In these circumstances schools will doubtless wish to:

- ensure continuity and progression for pupils' learning
- provide tuition of the highest quality
- ensure effective and efficient teaching

51

- provide regular monitoring and assessment of pupils' progress
- relate the instrumental music tuition to the general music curriculum.

The Music Forum strongly advises all schools to have, within their general policy, a clear statement on their provision for instrumental teaching and, where appropriate, a policy for remission of fees for tuition.

Support for the curriculum from professional musicians in schools

Gillian Moore

In recent years, schools have been encouraged by government to form links with industry and, indeed, to take on its language and culture. In more extreme manifestations (for example, City Technology Colleges), schools receive substantial financial sponsorship from industry; the sponsor's corporate logo can be embroidered on the blazer badge where a lofty Latin motto used to be, and headteachers have become chief executives. Elsewhere, even primary schools have their senior management teams, computer companies donate hardware for technology departments and business people and scientists can teach in schools under licensed teacher schemes.

But underneath the contemporary rhetoric, perhaps these ideas are not so new. In music teaching, there have been links with the industry for years, chiefly through instrumental teaching services. Many teachers working in the instrumental and vocal teaching services, particularly in large cities, earn part of their living teaching in schools and part of it playing or singing professionally. This regular and direct contact between pupils studying a subject in school and the cutting edge of its equivalent profession is unique to music, and one of the many benefits of a high quality instrumental teaching service.

A more recent and highly successful 'link with industry' has been through the education programmes which have been developed by professional orchestras, opera companies, jazz groups, world musicians, chamber ensembles and music festivals. In every region of Britain, major music organisations have highly developed programmes, and the music profession is able to provide encouragement, expertise and resources to support and develop music in schools, as well as in other areas of the community. Where at one time the music profession's involvement in education seldom went beyond 'concerts for schools', performers and composers can now be involved directly in work in the classroom, with extended curricular activities and in teacher in-service training, and projects involve primary, secondary and special schools. Most major orchestras, festivals and opera companies now have specialist education officers, and projects are tailored to fit with curriculum concerns of composing and performing, listening and appraising. Performers and composers often visit schools in preparation for concerts and perform-ances, which are no longer simply passive experiences for pupils, but are often the culmination of a longer process in which they have had a creative involvement. Most excitingly, the partnership between the music profession and schools is, in the best instances, a two-way process that can influence and change the music profession as much as it can support teachers in delivering the music curriculum: concerts are be-coming more flexible, welcoming experiences and musicians are devel-oping new performing, composing and communication skills in order to work in schools.

What are the benefits?

So what can professional musicians offer in schools which cannot be provided in day-to-day teaching, and how can these resources best be used?

In the professional development of teachers, there are many and obvious benefits in working directly with professional musicians.

For teachers

- There is support for and confirmation of the work which the teacher is already doing – music teaching can be a lonely business, and there can be nothing like the effect of a stranger coming into the classroom and saying what the teacher has been saying all along!
- Teachers can also benefit from having contact with people who are working at the cutting edge of the profession, allowing generalist primary teachers to gain new skills in developing music activities for pupils, and allowing specialist teachers to keep abreast of new devel-opments in the profession in particular areas in which they may lack expertise – for example, in composing, technology, world music or vocal work.
- Professional performers and composers can also provide help for teachers in dealing with pupils with special educational needs, either by providing the musical resources to allow pupils with disabilities to express their musical ideas or, just as importantly, providing fresh input for pupils who are specially gifted.

For pupils

- There is the opportunity to be in close contact with real excellence in performing – just noticing how professional instrumentalists sit, how they move, how they frame their performance with stillness and silence, how they take risks ('I never knew a clarinet could sound so loud, so quiet, so high ... '). This must have a positive effect on pupils' own performing, even on a classroom percussion instrument.
- Visiting composers can develop pupils' confidence in composing by introducing new compositional languages, structures and processes – for example, a composer may show how to transform a simple musical phrase composed by a pupil by playing it in a different mode, by systematically altering the rhythm, by cutting it up, playing it backwards.
- Pupils often have their compositional imaginations liberated by creating music for performers whose skills exceed those normally found in the classroom – a pupil may, for the first time, know what it is to create really fast music, or to hear something played genuinely loud.
- Notation can be part of the process too – there is no greater incentive for learning to write musical ideas down than if it is for a professional performer on his or her next visit.
- Professional projects often give pupils the opportunity to experience, some for the first time, the emotional impact of a live performance and, because of the detailed preparation which they have undergone, to view that performance with a heightened degree of involvement, knowledge and critical awareness.
- There is also a vocational dimension: when pupils meet people who earn their living in music, they will find out, for example, that composers are not exclusively elderly and male, that orchestras need administrators, that opera companies need technicians and that pop groups need road managers.

What is available?

Most major symphony orchestras, opera companies and ensembles offer education programmes, as do a great many smaller groups and individual musicians of all styles and cultures, including jazz, pop, traditional and folk music. Some concert venues have education policies based on their artistic programme, as have many major music festivals. Some local authorities and Regional Arts Boards make professional musicians available to schools through locally organized residencies for composers, performers and ensembles and in some cases individual schools or consortia of schools have organized and funded their own schemes. Specialist national organisations offer programmes in their particular field – for example, the Regional Jazz Organisations, Sonic Arts Network (music technology) and the Performing Right Society (Composers in Education Scheme).

Making it work

For professional musicians in the classroom to be a successful enterprise, everybody must be quite sure of their respective roles in the situation. The professional musicians must be an enhancement of existing teaching and not a replacement for it. The relationship between teacher and visitors is crucial, and works best when it is a genuine partnership in which each understands the other's strengths and limitations. Projects have been known to fail when the professional musician is expected to be willing and competent enough to do everything, and teachers have been diffident about offering their own specialist skills. The teacher is the educational professional, the person who knows the pupils and who has overall responsibility for them before, during and after the project. The visiting musician, however gifted a communicator (and they may not be) is able to offer something quite different – a very particular and specialized skill. Sometimes that 'very particular skill' can be as simple as the wonderful sound which a top-class violinist makes, or the virtuosity of an Indian musician or the voice of an opera singer. The teacher should, through careful involvement in the planning process, have influence over how that skill is directed for the greatest benefit to the pupils.

Planning is therefore crucial, and it is important that senior management of schools is involved in this process as well as the class or subject teacher. This means that the project will be adequately supported within the school and that practical considerations of timetabling, clashing examinations, school lunches and extra spaces will be addressed from the top down. It is also important that mutual expectations are made clear at the start, and this often involves a contract between the visiting organisation or individual and the school, outlining responsibilities and roles.

Funding

Although local management of schools (LMS) allows schools to choose to fund professional musicians in education schemes if they so wish, the work often does not have to be paid for in full by the individual schools involved. In some cases, the fees of the musicians have already been paid, through animateur, musician-in-residence and ensemble in residence schemes. Many orchestras, opera companies, ensembles and festivals now receive part of their core funding for education work and **55** are able to raise additional funds from sponsorship, statutory bodies or grant-making trusts. Some local education authorities have funds set aside specifically for professional musicians in schools and other money may be available through curriculum development funds and in-service training for teachers. Local authority arts departments are a possible source of funding, often through their budgets for festivals and special events, and visiting professional musicians can be an incentive for local companies to become involved in sponsorship. All Regional Arts Boards have funds to support the work of professional artists in education, and the Arts Council provides support principally through its touring programme and the Educational Development Fund.

Finding the information: useful organisations and publications

British Music Education Yearbook (Rhinegold)
Provides a full list of organisations and individual musicians (chiefly classical and jazz) who offer educational programmes together with short descriptions of the programmes offered. Also gives names and addresses of useful organisations, such as Arts Councils, Regional Arts Boards and specialist music organisations.

Musicians go to school
Survey and discussion of London Music organisations education work. Many of the organisations featured have a national remit and work all over Britain. London Arts Board (Public Affairs Department, tel: 0171 240 1313), January 1993, David Pratley Gwynn Rhydderch and John Stephens.

Music Teacher (Rhinegold)
Monthly publication containing occasional reports and articles about professional projects in schools.

The Association of British Orchestras
The ABO is able to provide information on the telephone about orchestras offering education programmes throughout Britain. Contact: Libby MacNamara on 0171 828 6913.

The Performing Right Society
29/33 Berners St, London W1P 4AA, tel: 0171 580 5544. The PRS will provide information about the Composers in Education scheme.

Regional Jazz Organisations
The British Music Education Yearbook provides a list of these, as well as a list of organisations throughout the country who organize educational projects.

Regional Arts Boards

There are fourteen Regional Arts Boards in England and Wales (The Scottish Arts Council provides this function in Scotland and the Northern Ireland Council in Northern Ireland). The RABs have responsibility for subsidising most arts organisations in England and Wales, although the Arts Council of England continues to support some of the larger organisations. All RABs have music or performing arts officers and some have education officers. All should be able to give information on local professional musicians and organisations offering education programmes. Names and addresses in the British Music Education Yearbook.

Arts Councils

- Arts Council of England, 14 Great Peter St, London SW1P 3NQ, tel: 0171-333 0100. Contact: Maggie Semple, Director of Education and Training.
- Arts Council of Scotland, 12 Manor Place, Edinburgh EH3 7DD, tel: 0131-226 6051. Contact: Matthew Rooke, Music Officer.
- Arts Council of Wales, 9 Museum Place, Cardiff CF1 3NX, tel: 01222 394711. Contact: Roy Bohana MBE, Music Director.
- Northern Ireland Council, 185 Stranmills Road, Belfast BT9 5DU, tel: 01232 381591. Contact: Philip Hammond, Music Director.

Sponsors, trusts and links with the business world

Julian Smith

Many businesses and charitable trusts give support to education in general and a fair number specifically support the arts including music; indeed music is one of the more popular areas for support. Reasons for giving support vary enormously, ranging from pure altruism to the gaining of publicity. Many businesses see it as increasingly important for them to support the community in which they operate in order to be, and be seen to be, good citizens. Support given to music education by businesses will often be considered by them within the context of their overall community programme. Charitable trusts, while primarily functioning from an altruistic standpoint, are nonetheless governed by trust deeds which define and control the causes to which they can give.

Support for music education comes in a wide variety of forms and covers an ever increasing range of activities. Some support goes directly from companies to schools in a number of different ways:

- gifts of cash
- donations in kind such as instruments and equipment

57

- secondments of staff with relevant useful knowledge, almost always on a part-time and occasional basis
- provision or loan of facilities such as transport, use of halls or conference rooms or advertising space in retail shops for activities such as school concerts.

Such support will come mainly on a local basis from companies based on or operating in the immediate locality of a school; it will less frequently come from charitable trusts unless they have a specifically regional or local remit. (How to set about raising direct business and trust support is dealt with below.)

A more significant way in which business, industry and trusts support music in schools is through sponsoring educational musical activities and events. These are put on by, on the one hand, professional musicians or musical organisations such as ballet or opera companies and, on the other hand, by charitable and other organisations specifically concerned with encouraging both the performance and appreciation of music by young people. The majority of orchestras, opera companies and ballet companies, particularly those that regularly go on tour, have educational programmes directed at schools.

The 1993/94 report of the Association for Business Sponsorship of the Arts (ABSA), published in November 1994, lists over 100 instances of sponsorship or support given to events, projects, competitions and so on, which were closely or directly connected with music education. The list is by no means comprehensive as not all companies are members of ABSA and a number of cases of support go unreported. The amount of support given by industry to music education is considerable and growing. It is seen by companies as a way of putting back into the community something of what they take out. From the point of view of business the sponsorship of aspects of music education is a fairly low key and relatively altruistic exercise. While it will certainly seek some form of reasonable recognition it is not normally looking for the high profile exposure that would be attracted by the sponsorship of a major sporting event with the television coverage that goes with it.

The range of activities involving music education and attracting sponsorship from business and industry is growing all the time and includes such things as:

- special concerts and performances for young people
- workshops and master classes put on for schools by orchestras, opera companies, ballet companies and individual performers both from their home bases and on tour
- competitions to encourage higher standards of performance and to recognize achievement
- subsidized ticket prices for concerts, performances and other events

- events to encourage the young to perform in public and to provide schools with a platform for their groups, orchestras and other performers
- bursaries and management support for young musicians at the start of professional careers
- direct provision of all sorts of musical instruments, electronic aids, practice and performance facilities and teacher support
- composers working in educational situations.

While the value of support to music education from business and industry should not be under-estimated it should never be relied upon as a mainstream source of funding. It is a valuable source of both money and expertise but is liable to fluctuate to a considerable extent in relation to the health of the nation's economy and to the changing needs of the businesses concerned. In any case most businesses will not be prepared to provide support for an open ended period of time. If they can be persuaded to commit themselves for, say, three years there is a strong probability that at the end of that period, they will decide that it is time to move on and devote their resources to some other good cause. Support from this sector must always be regarded as a useful and highly desirable bonus rather than as a permanent and certain source of support. Business and industry will always have the wish to support music education but may not always have the means.

Charitable trusts are less subject to the ups and downs of the economy although they are not immune to them. While it is often more difficult to attract their interest in the first place, they may sometimes be more amenable to longer term support although this will have to be reapplied for on a regular basis, often in competition with other applicants. Trusts too will eventually want to move their giving around to give other worthy causes a chance, so even they cannot be relied on for very long term giving.

Making direct applications

It is important to remember the old military maxim, 'Time spent on reconnaissance is seldom wasted'. Before any application for help is submitted to a business or a charitable trust it is vital to do your homework. There is nothing more frustrating or, for that matter, time wasting than spending a lot of effort in putting together an application only to find that the organisation to whom you submit it 'never gives to causes like that'.

Below are the important things to find out about an organisation you want to approach.

- What is their giving policy? Are there particular areas upon which they concentrate? How are these defined? Are some areas of endeavour or types of organisation specifically excluded from receiving gifts or grants?
- Who are the key people in the organisation? Do you know any of them; do you have access to them through friends, colleagues or contacts? In businesses these could be the directors of the company, the company secretary, the charity or sponsorship manager. For charitable trusts they would be the director of the trust, the trustees and the person who set up the trust.
- Who is the main decision making body for grants and how often, and when, does it meet?
- What sort of submission does it like to have? Should it be long/short, detailed/broad-brush, short but supported by appendices? How far ahead of a meeting should it be sent in?
- Is it possible to make a face-to-face presentation? This can often be very effective provided that it is supported by the appropriate paperwork. Unfortunately most organisations will not allow this but it is worth trying.
- What sort of acknowledgement do organisations require by way of publicity or other return?

There are a number of publications which you will find helpful in your research. The *Directory of Grant-Making Trusts* is published by the Charities Aid Foundation. The *Directory of Social Change* publishes, amongst other things, 'A guide to company giving', 'A guide to the major Trusts' and 'The Arts funding guide'. At least some of these should be available in your local library.

The ABSA is concerned with putting together potential business sponsors and arts organisations needing support and would certainly be prepared to give advice to any school seeking support.

Having found out all you can about the organisation to which you are applying it is necessary to put together a number of factors about yourselves which will be needed to support the application.

- Give a description of your school and its involvement in the community and, in particular, what it offers in the field of arts in general and music specifically.
- List any particular achievements in the musical and arts field which would add strength to your application.
- Be clear about what you are asking for. Is it money and, if so, how do you plan to spend it? If it is other resources, what exactly do you need and why? Is it a one-off need or is it ongoing?
- Be able to evaluate the use to which you have put the gift in some meaningful way, so as to reassure the giver that you have received

real value from their gift. This is particularly important if you are likely to want to make a follow-up application.

- Think about how to acknowledge the gift publicly so as to provide some payback for the donor. This may not always be necessary or appropriate but must be considered.
- Be prepared to receive visits from representatives of the donor organisation so that they can assess on the spot what you are doing with their gift.

Other support

A number of organisations, both business and charitable, do not provide direct support to individual schools. Rather they provide help by supporting the educational programmes of orchestras, opera and ballet companies particularly when they are on tour. These programmes cover such things as special performances for schools, subsidized tickets for ordinary performances, workshops and master classes.

It is certainly worth enquiring of local orchestras, opera companies and ballet companies if they have an educational programme and, if so, how you can benefit from it. Also keep an eye on the local press for advance notices of major musical organisations on tour who may be visiting your area. It will be well worth asking them if they plan to put on any events for young people and how you might be able to get involved.

In the field of providing a platform for young people to perform, Music for Youth, which is supported by a number of major companies, holds Regional Festivals for 50,000 young people each spring of whom about 7,000 go on to perform in the National Festival of Music for Youth in the South Bank complex in London in the summer. This is followed by three Schools Prom concerts in the Royal Albert Hall in November, which usually play to packed houses. During the National Festival there is a session specifically aimed at schools, teachers and school governors to provide advice and a forum concerned with the implementation of the Key Stages in the music curriculum. Music for Youth is based at Blade Mews, Deodar Road, London SW15 2NN.

Other possible sources of support are constantly arising. A recent example is the National Lottery. Currently its proceeds are available only for capital projects, and require 'partnership funding' – matching or additional funds which have already been earmarked to a project.

Seeking support from businesses, trusts or musical organisations for musical activities in or for schools can be enormously rewarding and provide a real boost for music in education. It is not always easy and you have to be prepared for disappointments; however it is tremendously worthwhile and perseverance will succeed in the long run. **61**

6 Progression and assessment

Kevin Adams, David Adams, Linda Read, John Stephens

Before discussing the implications of the new Orders for music in the area of assessment it will be helpful to consider a few basic questions. Firstly, what is meant by assessment? Secondly, why is assessment needed? Thirdly, what is to be assessed?

The simple answer to the first question is that assessment is a means of judging what pupils know, understand and can do. In practice assessment has become linked very closely with recording and reporting, and the importance of linking these three activities should certainly not be underestimated. It is very important to recognize, however, that there is a need to assess for purposes other than reporting; in fact, assessment should be seen as an integral part of the teaching and learning process.

The most immediate answer to the second question is, assessment is needed because there is a statutory requirement on schools to report to parents the 'strengths and targets for improvement' in all of pupils' work – of which music is a part. There is, though, no specific statutory requirement to assess music at present. It has been proposed that teachers might be required to assess pupils in music at Key Stage 3. If this is introduced, the earliest likely date for it would be September 1997.

However, educationally the most important reason for assessing is to inform the teaching and learning process – formative assessment. There is a need to know as much as possible about each pupil's ability in each aspect of a subject in order to be able to plan appropriate future learning activities. Clearly teachers need to be aware of pupils' strengths and weaknesses so that they may develop the former and remedy the latter. This **formative assessment** is an essential aid to ensuring **progression** through the curriculum.

A third reason for assessing pupils' achievements is to be able to provide accurate and detailed information about pupils' current levels of achievement, **summative assessment**, to all interested parties, for example the pupils themselves, parents, headteachers, governors and inspectors. In addition teachers need to assess in order to evaluate the effectiveness of their own schemes of work and teaching.

These reasons for assessing apply equally to all subjects in the curriculum. At one time it was believed by some teachers and educationalists that assessment in music was neither possible nor even desirable. It is now generally agreed that effective assessment is as essential in music as in any other subject area. We aim to show that it is also entirely practical for it to take place without burdening teachers with an unacceptable workload.

The third question – what is to be assessed? – has already been partly answered: clearly it is pupils' knowledge, skills and understanding which must be assessed. In that these are developed in music through the three distinct activities of performing, composing and listening, then assessment in the subject may relate to each of these activities. This point needs, perhaps, to be clarified here. In planning teaching it is vital that the three activities are linked – as has been stressed in all National Curriculum music documents from the outset. However, for assessment purposes the three may at times need to be viewed as separate – it is quite possible that pupils will have reached different stages in each of the three. Note that the three activities apply equally to the National Curriculum Order for England with its two Attainment Targets and the Order for Wales with its three:

Activity	NC England	NC Wales
Performing	AT 1 (Performing and Composing)	AT 1 (Performing)
Composing	AT 1 (Performing and Composing)	AT 2 (Composing)
Listening	AT 2 (Listening and Appraising)	AT 3 (Appraising)

It is also essential to recognize that there are some aspects of musical experience which may simply not be revealed in such a way that they can be assessed. For instance, the fact that a young pupil may not have developed a vocabulary to express an emotional or aesthetic response does not mean that the response has not taken place. Neither should the search for a means of assessing it lead to artificial tests or the unbalancing of programmes of musical study.

The National Curriculum Orders and assessment

Ever since the decision was taken in 1990 that music, art and physical education should have a different system of assessment and reporting from the other National Curriculum subjects there has been considerable debate on this matter. Whatever the arguments may be, we now have to accept that in music there are not to be the eight level descriptions used in most other National Curriculum subjects. All assessment must **63** consequently be based on the statutory Programmes of Study (PoS) and End of Key Stage Descriptions (EKSD).

The other main difference between music and the core subjects as regards assessment is that in music there will be no statutory externally set tests. This decision has been almost universally welcomed!

The Orders set out Programmes of Study and End of Key Stage Descriptions for each of the three Key Stages (as well as additional EKSD to reflect exceptional performance at Key Stage 3). The End of Key Stage Descriptions – as their name suggests – should be used only for **summative** assessment and reporting at the end of each Key Stage. All **formative** assessment for the purposes of monitoring progression should be based on the Programmes of Study. For this reason it is the Programmes of Study which we discuss first.

Formative assessment

The Task Group on Assessment and Testing (TGAT) report (the document which introduced the initial concept of ten levels of attainment), made a clear statement about the relationship of assessment to teaching and learning.

> The assessment process itself should not determine what is to be taught and learned. It should be the servant, not the master, of the curriculum. Yet it should not simply be a bolt-on addition at the end. Rather, it should be an integral part of the educational process, continually providing both 'feedback' and 'feedforward'.

> TGAT, A Report, paragraph 4

In the new Orders the role of the Programmes of Study has been strengthened. In addition to defining the knowledge, understanding and skills to be taught, these are now also intended to guide day-to-day formative assessment of pupils' work. This certainly makes the integration of assessment into the teaching and learning process much easier.

Unfortunately that does not solve all the problems: since the Programmes of Study have to be taught to all pupils at a particular Key Stage it is clear that strategies such as ticking statements as having been completed will be of little or no assistance in attempting to measure accurately the achievements of individual pupils. As we know, pupils learn musical skills and understanding through a process of continually revisiting skill areas and tasks. At any given point in time some pupils may just about be able to demonstrate basic competence in a particular skill or task while others may show a very high level of achievement.

What is needed, therefore, is some way of measuring how well pupils have achieved the demands of the Programmes of Study – as stated earlier, we need to identify strengths and weaknesses. In order to do this, we will need to supplement the Programmes of Study with further information giving details of the attainments of individual pupils.

The End of Key Stage Descriptions in the new (1995) Orders are intended to be clearly indicative of particular levels of achievement.

> The following [end of Key Stage] descriptions describe the types and range of performance the majority of pupils should characteristically demonstrate by the end of the Key Stage, having been taught the relevant Programme of Study. The descriptions are designed to help teachers judge the extent to which their pupils' attainment relates to this expectation. The expectations match the level of demand in other subjects and are broadly equivalent to level 2 at Key Stage 1, level 4 at Key Stage 2 and level 5/6 at Key Stage 3.

The EKSDs are now written in continuous prose to encourage a holistic approach to end-of-key-stage assessment as opposed to a box-ticking exercise.

In that the EKSDs now relate more clearly to particular levels, then they could be seen as being effective tools for assessment. They are, however, less precise compared with other subjects as they do not provide a statutory means of demonstrating achievement above or below the prescribed levels. For example, at Key Stage 1 any pupil failing to achieve the EKSD (set at level 2) cannot be shown to be at level 1, as can be shown in other subjects. On the other hand, the new EKSDs provide a Key-Stage-based bench-mark against which all pupils can be seen either to be working towards that goal, to have achieved it or to be working beyond it. This means that there is no risk that pupils, having given all they can to music at Key Stage 3, will be awarded an effective 'fail' grade of level 2.

Criteria for assessing achievement

If we are to assess how well a particular task has been completed it is important that we establish clear criteria on which to base our judgements. The criteria which we apply might include some of the following.

Performing:
    a Controlling sounds ... (Curriculum paragraph 4a)
        clarity and accuracy of pitch, rhythm and dynamics
        expression
        fluency
        technical control
        stylistic awareness.
    b Performing with others ... (Curriculum paragraph 4b)
        sense of ensemble

Composing:

a Composing in response to stimuli ... (Curriculum paragraph 4c)
organisation
expression
consistency.

b Communicate musical ideas ... (Curriculum paragraph 4d)
suitability of material
control of material
control of medium
originality.

Listening and Appraising:

a Listen, and develop understanding ... (Curriculum paragraph 4e)
accuracy in recognition and discrimination
amount of detail observed
soundness of judgements based on knowledge and understanding.

b Respond and evaluate ... (Curriculum paragraph 4f)
personal emotional and aesthetic response to music.

In all cases these criteria need to be considered in relation to the nature and level of difficulty of the task set. They need to be clearly understood by both pupils and teachers, accepted as reasonable, and capable of unambiguous interpretation in operation.

This is all very well, but we must also remember that, if assessment is to be a normal classroom activity, then judgements will need to be made quickly. There will be no time in practice to check against lists of criteria; rather the teacher will need to have a clear understanding of those criteria in order to make accurate 'on the spot' judgements. Consequently teachers will need to be clear about the specific learning objectives of each lesson taught – while recognising also the possibility of unexpected insights.

Assessing and recording pupils' achievements

On some occasions judgements made about pupils' performance will be put to use immediately, for example in deciding the nature of the next task to be undertaken in the same lesson. On many other occasions, however, this will not be the case; the information may not be used until the following lesson or some later date. There is clearly a need, therefore, to devise some way of recording the judgements made.

Marks or grades may have a part to play, but they will need to be supported by further details if they are to provide the information which is required about pupils' strengths and weaknesses.

The levels which form the basis of statutory assessment in most other
National Curriculum subjects could provide an alternative method of

assessing and recording pupils' attainment. Although these levels were never intended as a statutory form of assessment in music they have always been available – firstly in the final report of the Music Working Group, later in the non-statutory guidance provided by the Curriculum Council for Wales. These statements in one form or another may be helpful in supplementing the End of Key Stage Descriptions but they are not precise enough to provide much assistance in making day-to-day formative assessments of specific pupils' achievements.

The Music Working Group final report states the following.

Assessment should be simple and part of the classroom process, thus making only reasonable demands on time.

Music for *Ages* 5 to 14, DES and Welsh Office, 1991, paragraph 9.7

Teachers will, then, need to devise schemes of assessment which are efficient, yet practical within the heavy demands on their time.

In planning their record-keeping, teachers will need to bear in mind their own schemes of work and also the requirements of their school assessment policy. Marks or grades can be conveniently recorded in a traditional teacher's mark book. Some teachers find a need for more detailed descriptive information for which they have developed appropriate recording systems. All systems need to allow information to be transferred easily if, for example, a pupil moves to a different class (or school).

When to assess

Teachers assess pupils constantly in their classroom. They are not only concerned with musical achievements and learning, but also with relationships, motivation and patterns of behaviour. These judgements then form the basis of decisions about the appropriate tasks which will take individual pupils on to the next stage of their development. Such assessments are made within the usual flow of interactions in the classroom. They are rarely formalized, and may very well not be incorporated into the process of monitoring pupils' progress, although significant factors may be important to note and record. This **formative** mode of assessment is appropriate throughout the whole of the teaching/learning process.

Sometimes it is appropriate to use a **summative** style of assessment, for example at the conclusion of a task or a series of lessons.

Some formal assessments may be appropriate. For example, some teachers like their pupils to give a 'performance' at some time, pointing out that this is one aspect of the skill of performing. This is fine as long

... significant factors may be important to note and record

as it does not detract from the other parts of performing and as long as it does not take a disproportionate amount of teaching time.

Similarly in composing, the final product may be assessed, so long as due consideration is also given to the process of composing. This is particularly important with group composing where it is the attainment of each member of the group which needs to be assessed individually.

Appraising may also be assessed formally in relation to listening 'in audience', but chapter 2 makes clear that 'appraising' is deeply embedded in 'performing' and 'composing'. Only that part of it which is specifically concerned with 'listening in audience' is able to be assessed in isolation.

The formal testing referred to above may take place at the end of a unit of work and may thus test pupils' understanding arising from that unit. It often provides both a stimulus and a spur to learning, an opportunity to assess the stage reached and to report to parents.

Pupils' self-assessment

It is essential to involve pupils in the assessment of their own work. By assessing themselves they will be made aware of their own learning processes. Seeing how they view their achievements in a particular task can also be valuable to teachers in making their own assessments and in preparing future assignments. For example, it can be of great assistance in judging what individual pupils have contributed to and learned from a group composing project. The assessment of individual pupils' work within a group is one of the more difficult areas of assessment, and self-assessment can be invaluable in helping teachers to measure the depth of understanding gained by pupils whilst engaged in a particular task.

Retaining evidence

There is no statutory requirement that evidence of pupils' achievements in music be retained. It is desirable, however, that some evidence should be kept for a variety of reasons. Firstly, this may be used to support judgements made when reporting to parents. Secondly, it will be needed when undertaking moderation of standards – either between different teachers at a school or between different schools. Thirdly, it may be required by school inspectors.

Moderation

The fact that music is a subject which is entirely teacher-assessed is to be welcomed. This allows flexibility to reflect the differences – social, **69**

... essential to involve pupils in the assessment of their own work

geographical, ethnic – between schools across the country. It also presents challenges, however, as far as setting similar standards in all schools is concerned. It will be desirable for some form of moderation of standards to be undertaken. Schools in 'clusters' are already organising their own schemes of mutual moderation.

Distinctive features affecting assessment in music

One of the distinctive features of music is that large numbers of pupils undertake activities in the subject in addition to those done in class. Where possible recognition should be given to achievement in music:

- in instrumental lessons
- in extra-curricular activities at school
- in musical activities outside school.

Furthermore achievement in music should:

- recognize the often non-linear development of pupils
- reflect process as well as product
- not depend on oral ability or writing skills.

Assessment at Key Stages 1 and 2

Teachers of primary school pupils are familiar with undertaking assessments in all subjects. They can therefore draw strength from the fact that there are similarities between music and other subjects when it comes to assessment.

- Organisation will affect outcome.
- Resources will affect outcome.
- Planning for learning will affect outcome.
- Assessment may not be carried out with the whole class at the same time, even though all pupils may be doing the same activity.
- Judgements are based on professional understanding and knowledge.
- Assessments by the teacher are made by observing, listening, questioning and discussing, and involvement in/sharing the activity.
- Most importantly, any assessment made will be based on clear criteria. The criteria for assessment will affect how the assessment is made.

Assessment in music will need to take into account the following factors:

Organisation

- Will the whole class do music at the same time? If so, will they all do the same musical activity?

71

- Will the pupils work independently of each other?
- Will the pupils work in pairs, or in groups? How will pairs or groups be chosen?
- Is there time for the pupils to make music other than in a music lesson?

Resources

- What amount of time is available?
- What is needed in the way of equipment – instruments, recording material, and so on?
- Can the organisation of resources reflect a pupil's understanding of their appropriate use?

Planning

- Have the appropriate activities been provided in order for the pupil to be fairly assessed? (This applies before and during the assessment being made.)
- Will the activities be teacher-led?

Whom to assess

- Who is being assessed? How many?
- Will the assessment take place over a short or long period of time, e.g. during one lesson or during a half-term's unit of work?

How to assess

Which strategies for assessment are appropriate?

Strategies for assessment in music will include the following:

Observing

Opportunities to observe a pupil's musical behaviour present themselves in and out of music lessons. Things to look out for include:

- spontaneous musical activity
- response to music being heard
- readiness to listen to music – either performed live or taped
- type of involvement in a musical activity – is it always the same?

Listening to pupils' music

As pupils make music we can learn much about their musical under-standing and development. Application of their understanding to prac-tical tasks may be explicitly musical (as in composing or performing) or implicitly related to music (as in dance).

Listening to pupils' talk

Pupils also reveal much about their understanding and development when talking about music. The words they use and the way in which they use them can give an insight into what they see, hear, think, feel and know. Their talking may arise from purposeful teacher-led discus-sion or questioning or from incidental talk with another person.

Teacher involvement

As a result of being involved in a pupil's musical activity, the teacher can manipulate the situation so that the pupil reveals his/her musical understanding and development. This teacher involvement also allows for differentiation by task as well as by outcome.

Scenario
Key Stage 1   Year 1

Focus for teaching
Understanding of a steady beat.

Intended outcome
Pupils copying and/or devising their own steady beat actions. NB Even with a whole class it is usually easy during this activity to spot the pupils who do not feel a steady beat.

Organisation
Teacher and pupils sit in a circle.

Resources
Twenty minutes.
Taped music with a clear, steady beat.

Planning
A previous lesson introduced the musical concept of 'steady beat'. This lesson will give the pupils the chance to reveal their understanding through response and talk.

Activity

1 Teacher to ask 'Who can tell me anything about a steady beat?'
2 To taped music, pupils to respond with their own steady beat actions.
3 Teacher or teacher-chosen pupil to lead the rest of the class with their own steady beat actions.
4 Other pupil leaders to be chosen as appropriate.

Assessment opportunities
Responses to initial questions.
Use of musical language.
Individual action responses to steady beat music.
Performance skills.
Did anyone ask about when to stop/start?

Assessment strategies
Observing pupils' steady beat actions.
Listening to pupils' talk
Involvement – teacher initially leading by example but knowing when to allow others to lead.

Extension activity
In the music corner the pupils use a tape recorder to play a piece of music made up of sections with and without a steady beat. Their task is to put their own steady beat actions to the music.
What do they do during the section without a steady beat?

Understanding a steady beat

Scenario
Key Stage 2   Year 5

Focus for teaching
Understanding the stucture of ternary form – ABA.

Intended outcome
Pupils using ABA for structure in their own compositions and recognising it in the music of others.

Organisation
Pupils are in self-chosen groups.

Resources
Forty minutes.
Taped music of a piece with ABA structure, e.g. Grieg's 'Norwegian Dance'. Extensive range of tuned and untuned instruments.

Planning
During a previous lesson the same taped music was played and discussed in terms of its stucture and how that structure was achieved by the composer.
In this lesson the pupils will be given the chance to reinforce their understanding through talking and composing.

Activity
1   Pupils to listen to ABA piece.
2   Teacher to question pupils about the stucture.
3   Teacher to question how the pupils might compose in groups their own ABA piece.
4   Composing in groups.
5   Groups to perform in turn whilst others listen.
6   After each composition there will be opportunity to discuss the effectiveness of each piece.

Assessment opportunities
Responses to initial question.
Use of musical language.
Verbal and musical response to composing task.

Performance skills, e.g. control of sounds, keeping together.
Verbal responses made during discussion after each performance.

Assessment strategies
Observing – the role of each pupil involved in the process of his/her group's composition.
Listening – to pupils' talk.

75

Questioning – initial question and others as appropriate.
Discussing – joining in as appropriate.
Involvement – in the process of composing as and when appropriate.

Extension activity
Can each group of pupils compose other ABA pieces using alternative strategies, e.g. change of tempo, change of volume, effective use of instruments?

Assessment at Key Stage 3

Everything which has been described so far in connection with Key Stages 1 and 2 can also be applied at Key Stage 3. Additional factors arise from the different mode of organising music lessons for Key Stage 3, including instrumental tuition. A further factor already noted is the possible introduction sometime in the future of statutory assessment by teachers at Key Stage 3.

Performing

- This is likely to be assessed largely by means of informal classroom observation – not only in specific performing tasks but also often in composing activities.
- It is not necessary to make formal assessments of every pupil on each task, but records need to be kept of each pupil's development over a period of time.
- Performing activities both inside and outside the classroom should be included.
- The achievements of pupils can be differentiated both in the tasks which they are given and in the outcomes of a common task.
- Provision must be made to assess individual competence as well as ensemble awareness.

Composing

- Most compositions need to be assessed in the classroom. This is particularly important in the case of group compositions because of the need to identify the process and the contributions of individual pupils.
- It is ideas, structures, development and imagination which determine outcomes in composing work.

- Since time is of the essence it is important that curriculum plans build in appropriate assessment time and methodology.
- Pupils will often be engaged on basically the same task, with differentiation being achieved by outcome and by such factors as the amount of time and assistance allowed.
- It is almost always possible to make useful observations about performing and appraising skills during composing activities.
- Pupils' self-assessment will often be of great value.

Appraising

While conventional written or oral tests may have a place in the summative assessment of appraising skills, even at Key Stage 3, where a reasonable standard of articulacy can be expected, the assessment of appraising may very often involve a teacher being sensitive to a pupil's gesture or movement, to a pupil's creation of something in an art form other than music, to an achievement ostensibly in performing or composing. And, as the section on Appraising in chapter 2 makes clear, some appraising is simply invisible, as a musical concept or phenomenon is internalized in a way which is not open to verbalisation.

Keeping records

It may be helpful to keep a limited amount of exemplar material of various standards of work. This should include the work of a range of pupils together with teachers' notes showing agreed standards of performance, and illustrating the range of attainment of pupils throughout the Key Stage. Such work may promote staff discussion about assessment criteria and their development in the practical situation and will also serve as reference sources for new staff and as specific evidence for auditors and inspectors. The material should be clearly documented with information such as the date, class, resources available and used, background description, teacher input, and indications of pupils' strengths and of areas needing further work.

7 Materials for the classroom at Key Stages 1, 2 and 3

Christine Wood

The most vital resource for implementing the National Curriculum requirements for music is the teacher: abundant material resources presented without enthusiasm and preparation are a waste of precious schools funds. Valuable and exciting music education can be achieved with minimum resources by an inventive teacher.

But however charismatic teachers may be, sufficient resources are required to give them the confidence to plan well-balanced programmes of music education for the class or school.

KEY RESOURCE AREAS

Time

In a crowded curriculum the time allotted to music may seem inadequate. OFSTED recommends 5 per cent of time to be devoted to music in the primary school and at Key Stage 3. Extra time can be obtained in the following ways.

- Linking music with other subjects.
- Using 'blank' times, e.g., while waiting in line for assembly, practise a tricky line in a song.
- Linking listening and appraising activities with assembly listening time.

Space

Appendix 4 of the HMI document 'Music from 5 to 16' (HMI *Curriculum Matters 4: Music from 5 to 16*; HMSO 1985) provides guidance for recommended accommodation, but:

- seemingly inappropriate places can have positive benefits in allowing pupils to hear sounds in different acoustics – e.g. cloakroom, cupboard, corridor, outside.

Human resources

Use the special interests and experiences of other teachers, friends, pupils' families, other schools, local amateur and professional musicians in groups and individually.

Radio and television

The inherent passivity of broadcasts needs to be balanced with practical preparation and follow-up work.

Books and music

Build up as wide a variety as possible of materials for both teacher and pupils, including the following.

- Teachers' information books for syllabus and lesson planning.
- Progressive courses – but keep in mind individual pupils' different rates of learning, and the need to return to previous work to consolidate learning.
- Games and activities for re-inforcing learning of particular aspects of music.
- Songbooks chosen with the needs of the National Curriculum in mind, so that there is a variety of historical period, formal and informal style, geographical and cultural background and different types of accompaniment and unaccompanied songs.
- Instrumental music with and without voices and accompaniments.
- Pupils' reference books, including some of high quality – hard-backed and in full colour.

Instruments

Ensure that there are enough instruments for every pupil to have something to use in a class lesson. Also:

- check for safety and sturdiness, especially in 'home-made' instruments
- provide a variety in terms of pitch, tuned and untuned, method of sound making (blown, plucked, hit, electronic, acoustic), material of manufacture (wood, metal, plastic), ethnic origin
- encourage teachers and pupils to bring their own instruments of any kind
- arrange suitable storage for each type of instrument, e.g. rack or trolley, plastic boxes, cloth bags
- keep a stock of spare pins, rubber tubing for running repairs.

Recordings

Ensure a variety of vocal, choral and instrumental music, and also bear in mind:

- mood (e.g. exciting/calming)
- familiarity
- texture (solo and ensemble voices and instruments)
- male and female performers and composers
- geographical and cultural origin
- formal and informal styles
- historical period and contemporary music.

It is possible to make up your own tapes from broadcast music. (Check that your school or LEA is licensed for this.)

RECOMMENDATIONS FOR INSTRUMENTS AND EQUIPMENT

Full colour illustrated catalogues, available from your local music shop, are invaluable for identifying and pricing the great range of classroom instruments now available.

Key Stages 1 and 2

Classroom instruments

'Tuned' instruments

Chime bars – usually with metal bars:

- versatile, usable as a set, in groups or individually
- very good value, especially used with a variety of beaters
- minimum of six bars (C D E G A C¹).

Xylophones – wood, or wood substitute, bars:

- fibreglass bars are preferable for strength – check that wood bars are from replaceable hardwoods
- 'diatonic' means one row of bars equivalent to the white notes of a piano, but usually two extra bars are provided (F sharp and B flat, the most commonly used 'black' notes)
- a 'chromatic half' is available separately to link with a diatonic set to provide the 'black' notes
- soprano (smallest), alto and bass are the most widely available.

Glockenspiels – metal bars producing a bright ringing sound:

- diatonic and chromatic are available
- soprano and alto are the most commonly available.

Metallophone – metal bars producing a resonant sound:
- diatonic and chromatic are available
- soprano, alto and bass are most widely available.

Beaters – provide pairs of beaters with a variety of different heads (felt, wood, plastic, rubber).

Bass chime bars and/or bass xylophones and metallophones are important in providing a contrast to the many high sounding classroom instruments.

Steel pans may be available at a local music centre and are not beyond the scope of infants.

Gamelan instruments form a sophisticated percussion orchestra, and are visually and acoustically attractive. Some LEAs and university music departments have them, and versions exist made of scrap metal.

Tubular bells – these are expensive, but they give a unique sound and are visually appealing.

Keyboards

- **Piano and keyboard** can be used for dance and movement and for composing by all pupils (not just those having piano lessons).
- **Piano** is useful for pupils in composing because of the wide pitch range.
- **Small electronic keyboards** are quite cheap, but provide a limited choice of sounds and rhythms.
- **Larger keyboards** give many opportunities for sound production and experimentation, and can have sophisticated functions such as 'sampling', where a sound such as a tap running, can be recorded, and the sound then manipulated in various ways.

Harmonium – often used in Indian music.

Accordion – an interesting portable keyboard.

Recorders

- As these are wind instruments, they provide a contrast to percussion and keyboard sounds.
- **Descant** (soprano), **treble** (alto) and **tenor** are most suitable for this age group.
- They are traditionally used in ensemble and as accompaniment to singing, but encourage experimentation, such as using the mouthpiece alone.
- Ensure that the instrument is held correctly from the start – that is, right hand below the left hand.

Other wind instruments for sound variety

- Tin whistles, fifes, melodicas, pan pipes, swanee slide whistles, sirens, ocarinas, 'pea' whistles.
- Orchestral wind instruments may be brought in by pupils or their families, such as **flute**, **piccolo**, **oboe**, **clarinet**, **saxophone**, **bassoon** (important because it is low pitched).

Stringed instruments

- **Guitar, mandolin, banjo** – for chord accompaniments.
- **Autoharp**, **chordal dulcimer** – easy to play instruments for accompaniment.
- More sophisticated instruments such as **violin, viola, cello, double bass and sitar**, are all playable by primary pupils.

Brass instruments

- Some primary pupils may be learning **trumpet, cornet** or **tenor horn**.
- Older pupils may play **trombone, euphonium** or **tuba**.

'Untuned' instruments

Drums – tambour, tambourine, bongos, side drum, snare drum, tongue drums.

Metal instruments – e.g. cymbals of varying sizes, gongs, triangles, Indian bells, jingle bells.

Wood type instruments – e.g. castanets, claves, guiros, temple blocks, woodblocks, slap sticks, tone blocks.

Shakers – e.g. maracas, afuche, rain sticks.

Novelty instruments – e.g. animal sound effects.

Audio-visual equipment

Cassette recorder with counter – essential for recording pupils' experiments and compositions.

Portable cassette for mobile recordings.

Headphones for private listening and to avoid disturbing others.

Tape recorder (reel to reel) – useful for sound experiments.

TV, video recorder, video camera – for TV broadcasts, and for recording group work as an aid to assessment.

CD player – for high quality reproduction of listening material.

OHP and transparencies to project pupils' own scores, or purchased material.

Miscellaneous equipment

Metronome – fixed pulse indicator.
Tuning forks – also useful in science work.
Music stands – full size and desk size.
Music board, flip chart.
Computer and suitable **software**.

- In this fast-developing field, advice is available from secondary school music departments, LEA advisers and specialist retailers.
- Up to date information on what is currently available can be found in the British Music Education Yearbook.

Key Stage 3

As for Key Stages 1 and 2, plus:

- a range of electronic keyboards and linking equipment
- computer equipment – synthesizer, sampler, more advanced software, MIDI interface
- wider range of orchestral, band, ethnic and early instruments
- more sophisticated recording and playback facilities.

BOOKS AND PRINTED MUSIC

This is a selection only for Key Stages 1, 2 and 3, of titles mostly published within the last few years, based on recommendations from teachers and advisers. Full names and addresses of publishers can be found in the British Music Education Yearbook, published by Rhinegold Publishing Limited, 241 Shaftesbury Avenue, London WC2H 8EH.

Teachers should aim to use some titles from each category.

Symbols used:

Price range	Under £5	£
	Between £5–£10	££
	Between £10–£15	£££
	Over £15	££££
	Teacher's book	T
	Pupils' book	P
Key Stage – the main stage(s) covered (R=Reception)		R,1

Audio recording	CD 
Very little music literacy required	
Cross-curricular material	CC
Video available	V
Easy piano accompaniments	EP
Photocopiable material included	PC

Key to listing

1st line: Title
2nd line: Author
3rd line: Publisher

Teacher information: syllabus and lesson planning

Come on Everybody, Let's Sing
Lois Birkenshaw-Fleming

££££ R,1

Gordon V Thompson, Canada 07715 7252 2. (Available in UK from Lovely Music.)
- Comprehensive, clearly presented, very practical. Invaluable general resource.

Gently into Music
Mary York

£££ R,1 £££

Longman 0582 18673 0 (book) 0582 18672 2 (cassette)
- A highly recommended book and cassette, widely used, including information on progression and timing of activities.

Guide to Rock and Pop
Guide to Jazz, Folk, and Australian Music
Various authors

Each £££ 2,3,4

Science Press (Music Sales/Novello)
- Two books of useful information for teachers or pupils.

High Low Dolly Pepper
Veronica Clark

££ R,1,2 PC

A & C Black 07136 3329 8
- Activities and information on specific music elements. Photocopiable games pages.

Musical Knowledge
Keith Swanwick
Routledge 0415 10097 6

- A study of the relationship between intuition and analysis as we engage with music.

Music for Fun, Music for Learning
Lois Birkenshaw

Holt, Rheinhart and Winston third edition 003 921102 9
- Earlier, and much admired book by the author of *Come on Everybody Let's Sing*, with the same virtues.

Music in Action Key Stage 1

Music in Action Key Stage 2
Various authors
City of Wakefield Metropolitan District Council

- Ring file packed with activities clearly laid out.

Music in the Primary School revised edition
Janet Mills
Cambridge University Press 0521 38754 X

- A handbook for teachers covering all aspects of music teaching.

Music, Mind and Education
Keith Swanwick
Routledge 0415 01479 4

££

- An in-depth study of the sociological dimensions of musical experience.

Music: A Practical Teaching Guide
Science Press (Novello/Music Sales)

££   3,4

- Includes useful chapters on graphic notation, ostinato, form etc.

Sound and Structure
John Paynter
Cambridge University Press 0521 356776

£££   £££▣

- Creative music making − a rationale, and a guide to its technique. Book with accompanying cassette.

Take Note
Leonora Davies

BBC Educational Publishing 0563 35378 3

- A book and cassette with guidance on planning and implementing the music curriculum. The cassette has a variety of listening material.

What Primary Teachers Should Know About
Music

d'Reen Struthers
Hodder and Stoughton 0340 62124 9

- A comprehensive book with lesson ideas based on the musical elements, linked to the cassette. Includes teaching and planning information and a useful bibliography.

Women and Music

Aelwyn Pugh
Cambridge University Press 0521 34677 0

- The only book on this subject suitable for use in school. Written for pupils, but useful for teachers. Every teacher should have a copy.

Music courses

Active Music 1 and 2
Peter Dunbar-Hall and others
Science Press (Novello/Music Sales)
Teacher's books   Each   £££

Pupils' books   Each   £££   ▭

- A comprehensive book of more traditional music teaching ideas, with practical activities on all aspects of the curriculum. Part of a whole series of books from Australia.

First *Assignments*
David Tutt
Cambridge University Press
Pupils' book

Two cassette pack of musical
examples

- One of the 'Cambridge Assignments in Music' series, most of which are intended for Key Stage 4. This one contains 136 short assignments based on the elements of music.

Growing with Music (Somerset Music
Education Programme)
Michael Stocks and
Andrew Maddocks
Longman

Stage 1 (Key Stage 1):
Teacher's book   ££££

Cassette   ££

Evaluation pack (one of each teacher's and cassette) around £25.

Stage 2A (Key Stage 2, 7 to 9 years):
Teacher's book   ££££

Pupils' book 1   £

Pupils' book 2   £

Cassette   ££

Evaluation pack (one of teacher's and pupils' books, and cassette) around £29.

Stage 2B (Key Stage 2, 9 to 11 years):
Teacher's book   ££££

Pupils' book 3   £

Pupils' book 4   £

Cassette   ££

Evaluation pack (one of teacher's and pupils' books, and cassette) around £29.
- A song based course, using both sol-fa and ordinary notation in both the pupils' books and the teacher's books. Not for the faint-hearted.

Let's Make Music: Music for All
Topics for Key Stage 1
book and cassette

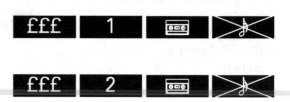

Let's Make Music: Music for All
Topics for Key Stage 2
book and cassette

Prill and Martin Hinkley
Novello/Music Sales

- Topic based activities, a little confusing in layout, but with lots of ideas.

Let's Make Music: Music for All
Topics for Key Stage 3 book and
cassette
Trevor Webb and David Leeke
Novello/Music Sales

- Ten topics such as syncopation, ostinati, with a cassette of all the music examples.

Lively Music 7–9
and
Lively Music 9–11
Wendy Hart
Heinemann Educational

- Each ringbinder costs around £70 and includes two cassettes plus a mass of resource material including detailed lesson plans, songs and worksheets from pupils. Published 1995 and 1996, so as yet untried.

Music All the Time

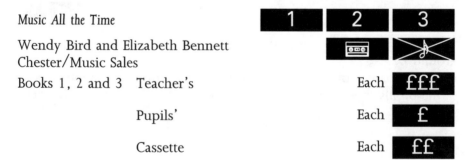

Wendy Bird and Elizabeth Bennett
Chester/Music Sales

Books 1, 2 and 3 Teacher's	Each	£££
Pupils'	Each	£
Cassette	Each	££

- Comprehensive progressive course, with lots of useful background information for teachers. The cassette is the weakest element.

Music Through Topics
Veronica Clark
Cambridge University Press

R,1 | ££ | £££ 🔊

- Teacher's book and cassette based on topics, but structured to provide a short course.

Nelson Music
Mary Edwards and
Lis Fletcher
Thomas Nelson
Nelson Music 1 (ages 5 to 7)
Nelson Music 2 (ages 7 to 9)
Nelson Music 3 (ages 9 to 12)

1,2 | T££££ | CD | 🔊

- Not yet published at the time of going to press. Each stage has a teacher's book, and a set of six cassettes (also available in CD format) at around £60.

Music File
Edited by Michael Burnett
Stanley Thornes

3,4 | 🔊 | PC

- A ring binder file of photocopiable material from many different contributors. Covers a wide variety of topics for pupils, with useful information for teachers, plus a cassette. Available each term on annual subscription of around £60.

Music Matters
Marian Metcalfe and Chris
Hiscock
Heinemann Educational

3,4 | 🔊 | PC

- A ringbinder file including three cassettes, costing over £70, but providing a mass of resource material including lesson plans, songs, accompaniments, worksheets, information for pupils etc. Advisers tend to complain at the exclusive use of this course.

Oxford Primary Music
Leonora Davies and
Jean Gilbert
Oxford University Press

R,1,2 | 🔊 | ✂✕

Key Stage 1 Teacher's pack

£££ | R,1

Pupils' books 1A (six in pack)

£££

Pupils' books 1B (six in pack)

£££

Cassette	££
Key Stage 2 Teacher's pack	£££ 2
Pupils' book 2 (six in pack)	£££
Cassette	££

- Published 1986 and 1989 respectively, but a detailed well constructed course, providing a good framework for progression.

Silver Burdett Music
English edition edited by
George Odam
Stanley Thornes

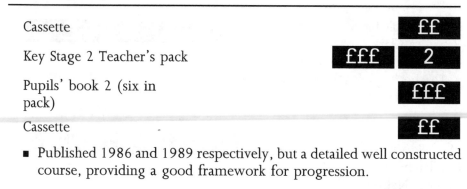

- A very expensive, beautifully produced, comprehensive course, but originally produced pre-National Curriculum. If funds are limited, remember you could buy a big bass xylophone for about the same price.

Sounds Topical
Jan Holdstock and
Christine Richards

Oxford University Press

Teacher's resource book	££££
Set of three different pupils' books	£££
Cassette pack (Song cassette and Listening cassette)	££££

Discount starter pack (teacher's book, four pupils' sets, cassette pack) around £70.

- Published 1995, so as yet untried. There are 75 topic based activities, and 40 linked listening extracts on cassette.

Targeting Music
Dorothy Taylor

R,1,2,3

Schott

Book 1 Reception	££
Book 2 Year 1	££
Book 3 Year 2	££

■ Not yet published at the time of going to press. Further volumes up to Year 7 in preparation.

Activities, projects and games

Creepy Crawly Book
Jan Holdstock
Lovely Music

■ Songs using minibeast names for rhythm activities. Excellent value at under £2.

Beaters series
Various authors
Schott

Each

■ Eleven books for teachers, based on Orff principles, by experienced authors. Some have cassettes.

Earwiggo 1, 2 and 3
Jan Holdstock and
Mavis West
Lovely Music

■ Listening, rhythm and pitch games in handy format at bargain prices. Essential starter books for teachers.

Everyday Music ('Ways into Music' series)
Christine Richards
Lovely Music and Christine Richards

■ Activities in dynamics, pitch and timbre.

Game Songs for Infants ('Ways into Music' series)
Christine Richards
Lovely Music and Christine Richards

■ Songs and activities to teach specific music skills.

Game Songs with Professor Dogg's Troupe
Edited by Harriet Powell
A & C Black

■ In the familiar oblong format, 44 fun songs with games and activities.

Sound Inventions
Richard McNicol
Oxford University Press

■ Thirty-two creative activities based on interesting and unusual starting points.

Sounds Fun 1 and 2
Trevor Wishart
Universal Edition

Each   **££**   **2,3**

- Two ever-popular pocket size books of games.

Sound Waves
Leonora Davies
HarperCollins

£££   **2**   **CC**

- Practical ideas including pupil workshop activities.

Songbooks

Big Book of Children's Songs
Eileen Diamond
IMP

££   **R,1**   **££**▣

- Mixture of action songs, rounds, some with instrumental accompaniment.

Birds and Beasts
Edited Sheena Roberts
A & C Black

££   **R,1**

- Familiar and new songs with games and activities, and with teaching notes.

Bobby Shaftoe Clap Your Hands
Sue Nicholls
A & C Black

££   **R,1**

- Reassuringly familiar songs with new words which help to teach musical concepts.

Earwiggo 4, 5 and 6
Jan Holdstock and
Mavis West
Lovely Music

£   **R,1**

Earwiggo 4 – Four chord book. Easy songs with simple chime bar accompaniments.
Earwiggo 5 – Five note book. Easy pentatonic songs.
Earwiggo 6 – DIY song book. New words for familiar tunes. Make up your own song for any topic.

- Handy starter song books, excellent value, packed with suggestions.

Eileen Diamond Super Songbooks 1 and 2
Eileen Diamond
Universal Edition

Book 1

Book 2

- Books with cassettes designed specifically for the National Curriculum (pre-1995). Book 1 includes movement and creative activities. Book 2 has part songs and percussion accompaniments.

Hubble-Bubble
Alison Hedger
Music Sales (Golden Apple)

- A mix of activities including starter ideas for the musical elements.

Hullabaloo-Balay
Arranged Barry Carson Turner
IMP

2,3

Teacher's book

Melody and percussion part

- Forty popular songs, some two part, with tuned and untuned percussion parts and guitar chords included in the pupils' book.

Junkanoo
Diana Thompson and Shirley Winfield
Universal Edition

- A book and cassette with a wide variety of interesting songs. The cassette 'flips over' from the song to the accompaniment on its own.

Look Lively, Rest Easy
Edited by Helen East
A & C Black

- A book and cassette of songs and stories of contrasting moods, and from different cultures. Includes teaching notes.

Our Street
Jan Holdstock
Lovely Music

£ **1**

- Songs useful for a local area topic, including opportunities for simple vocal improvisation.

Songpack
Ian Butler
Music Sales (Chester)
Teacher's book

3

££

Pupils' book (for voices and C instruments)

£

Instrument pack (three Easy recorder, three Tuned percussion, two Bb melody)

£££

Recorder/percussion pack (four Easy recorder, four Tuned percussion)

£££

- Good mixture of styles, with follow-up suggestions for listening and composing activities, with teaching notes.

Songs of England
Songs of Ireland
Songs of Scotland
Songs of Wales
Songs of the Americas
Songs of Christmas

Each

££

Caneuon Cymru (Welsh words and melody edition)

£££

Arranged Margery Hargest Jones
Boosey & Hawkes
- A useful collection of unison songs for all ages.

Turnip Head
Jan Holdstock
Lovely Music

£   **1,2**

- Songs and activities for the autumn term.

We Will Sing!
Doreen Rao
Boosey & Hawkes
Teacher's book

2,3

£££

Cassette

££

- A performance based music course imported from North America, where Doreen Rao has an almost charismatic following.

Whoopsy Diddly Dandy Dee
Diana Thompson and Shirley Winfield
Universal Edition
■ A book and cassette similar to *Junkanoo*.

Up, Up and Away
Derek Pearson
Oxford University Press
■ Fifty songs integrated with related poems, games, stories and movement.

Part songs for Key Stages 1 and 2

Easy Mix 'n' Match

Mix 'n' Match

More Mix 'n' Match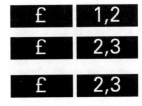
David Jenkins and Mark Visocchi
Universal Edition
■ Ever popular books of 'Partner' songs: an easy introduction to part singing using familiar songs.

Sing a Part 1 and 2   Each
Michael Stocks
Oxford University Press
■ Unaccompanied, well arranged two and three part songs in the 'Sing for Pleasure' series.

Round Up

Ten Million Green Bottles

Spinning Wheel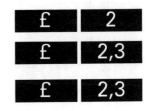
Jan Holdstock
Lovely Music
■ Three books of original rounds which work well, and have very amusing words.

Composing

Composing at the Electronic Keyboard Book 1
Nicholas Haines
Longman

- Two booklets for pupils to work from. Book 2 is for Key Stage 4.

Composing Demystified
Various authors
Curriculum Council for Wales

- A book and video pack of case studies based on twelve units of work. Linked to the Welsh curriculum, but equally applicable to other curricula.

Composing in the Classroom
Opus 1

Composing in the Classroom
Opus 2

David Bramhall
Boosey & Hawkes

- Group activities (not progressive), using classroom instruments.

Composing in the Classroom
Ruth Harris and Elizabeth Hawksley
Cambridge University Press

- A book for teachers on the place of composing in the curriculum, and how to organize it.

Recipe Book 1, 2 and 3
Jan Holdstock
Lovely Music

Book 1 – Grid notation

Book 2 – Chord boxes

Book 3 – Exploring and Scoring

- Three books of ideas for three different ways into composing.

Jazz in the Classroom
Eddie Harvey
Boosey & Hawkes

- A teacher's book, pupils' book and cassette to introduce improvisation using jazz techniques.

Listening and appraising

Composer's World
Wendy Thompson
Faber Music

Each

- Information books on Beethoven, Debussy, Haydn, Mozart, Schubert and Tchaikovsky, plus a separate project book.

Listening In 1, 2 and 3
William Salaman
Boosey & Hawkes

Three teacher's books

Each £

Three pupils' books

Each £

Three cassettes

Each £

- One of the first titles published on the subject, leading up to GCSE. Score reading, and questions to stimulate listening, from simple one stave melodies to full orchestral scores.

Oxford First Companion to Music
Kenneth and Valerie McLeish
Oxford University Press

2,3

Music Round the World

£

Instruments and Orchestras

£

The Story of Music

£

Composers and their Music

£

- Not new, but still very useful for background information for pupils (and teachers!).

Cross curricular titles

'Explore Music'
David Wheway and Shelagh Thomson
Oxford University Press

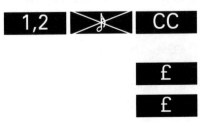

Explore Music through Art

£

Explore Music through Geography

£

Explore Music through History	£
Explore Music through Maths	£
Explore Music through Movement	£
Explore Music through Poetry and Rhyme	£
Explore Music through Science	£
Explore Music through Stories	£
Explore Music through Word Games	£
Explore Music – complete pack	££££

- A unique series of nine books of music activities linked to, and sharing techniques with other curriculum subjects.

Music and Family Life. Tudors,
Stuarts and Georgians
Alison and Michael Bagenal
Oxford University Press

| T£ | 2 | ££ 📼 | CC |

- A book and cassette providing material for music, dance, craft and drama.

'Music from the Past'
Alison and Michael Bagenal
Longman

| 2 | CC |

Medieval People	£ £££ 📼
Tudor England	£ £££ 📼
Stuart England	£ £££ 📼
The Victorians	£ £££ 📼

- Four books with accompanying cassettes with the usual Bagenal mix of activities.

The Green Umbrella
Jill Brand
A & C Black

| ££ | 2 | CC |

- Starting points for environmental topics: stories, songs and poems.

Sound and Music
Barbara Taylor
Kingfisher Books

£ | 2 | CC

■ Simple sound experiments from the 'Fun with Simple Science' series.

Story, Song and Dance
Jean Gilbert
Cambridge University Press

■ Ten stories, plus ideas for links with music, movement, and drama.

Cross Over to Music
Christine Richards
Lovely Music/Christine Richards

£ | 2 | CC

■ Music activities linked to the core subjects.

Three Singing Pigs
Kaye Umansky
A & C Black

££ | 1 | CC

■ Music activities based on traditional stories.

World music

Creating Music Round the World
Paul Sturman
Longman

■ Projects to start pupils composing and performing music in the styles of many countries.

Festivals
Jean Gilbert
Oxford University Press

■ A book and cassette providing information and activities based on thirteen festivals from around the world. Stories, songs, art and craft, recipes, and resource lists for books recordings, and useful addresses

Folk Songs from ...
... *Africa*
... *the British Isles*
... *the Caribbean*
... *Eastern Europe*
... *the Far East*
... *India*
... *Ireland*

... North America
... the Sea   Each

Faber Music
- Nine (so far) attractive books, some with percussion accompaniments and background notes.

Guide to the Gamelan
Neil Sorrell
Cambridge University Press
- An comprehensive information book for teachers.

Guide to Music Around the World
Peter Dunbar-Hall and Wendy Hodge
Science Press/Novello
- Includes information on less well-known countries. Useful for teachers and pupils. The cassette is a great asset.

Indian Music in Education
Gerry Farrell
Cambridge University Press
- An information book for teachers.

Instruments Around the World
Andy Jackson
Longman
- Listening, craft, writing and discussion ideas based on a specific instrument from a wide range of countries. The useful cassette is available from Sussex Tapes.

The Singing Sack
David Moses
A & C Black
- A book and cassette of 28 song stories with background information and ideas for activities.

Teaching Non-Western Music at Key Stage 2/3
Edited Chris Naughton
Rhinegold Publishing Ltd
- An extremely useful booklet of information and exercises on Chinese, Indonesian, African, Indian and Brazilian music. You can glean information on resources from the advertisements.

Special needs

'Earwiggo' series.
- These six books listed in the earlier sections 'Activities, projects and games', were produced for the Yorkshire and Humberside Association for Music in Special Education.

Pied Piper
John Bean and
Amelia Oldfield
Cambridge University Press

££ R,1

- Music activities to develop basic skills.

The Music Curriculum and Special Educational Needs
National Association of Special
Educational Needs (NASEN)

£

- A practical handbook with a four page list of suitable resources.

Up, Up and Away

££ R,1

- Previously listed under 'Songbooks', these songs were written especially for pupils with special needs.

Wonderful Me
Caroline Hoile
Music Sales/Golden Apple

T£ ££ R,1

- A book of ten songs involving body awareness and sensory perception.

Instrumental music for the classroom

Recorder tutors

Abracadabra Recorder
A & C Black

Each £ 1,2

- A series of nine books: Books 1 to 4 are for descant recorder, 5, 6, 8 and 9 include descant, treble, and tenor ensembles. Book 7 is a treble tutor. Some of the tunes are linked to songs in the A & C Black song book series.

Playtime
Margot Fagan
Longman
Teacher's book
Play Together (an ensemble book)

Each **£** **1,2**

- Ever popular, clearly presented course for young beginners. Stages 1 to 4 are for descant recorder, stages 5 and 6 are for treble.

Recorder from the Beginning
John Pitts
Thomas Nelson/Music Sales

Each **T££** **2**

Each **P£** **2**

Each **££**

- Three descant recorder books each with a teacher's book, plus three extra books of tunes. There is a separate treble book for teachers and pupils. A new edition includes three cassettes of the tunes and separate accompaniments.

Recorder ensemble

First Trios for Recorders

£

Folk Tunes for Recorders

£

Christmas Tunes for Recorders

£

Helen and Manton Dumville
Lovely Music/Manton Music

- Three books by experienced teachers for descant and treble recorders unaccompanied.

'Mimram Music'

Each **££**

Jane and Howard Gannaway
Fentone Music

- Many titles in a variety of styles for descant, treble and tenor recorders, some with piano accompaniments. Includes such titles as 'Waltz of the Sugar Plum Flower' and 'Lullaby of Birdland'.

'Bosworth Music for Recorders'
Bosworth

Each **£–££**

- A catalogue of interesting titles, mostly for descant, treble, tenor, and bass, including three Beatles selections.

Other publishers of classroom recorder music are: Schott, Universal Edition, Oxford University Press and IMP.

Classroom ensemble music

'Middle Eight Junior Music Kits'   Each 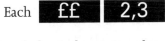 **££ 2,3**
Boosey & Hawkes
- More than 12 titles of popular, traditional and classical tunes, each in a plastic pack, providing sufficient parts for a whole class. A score and melody and harmony parts are included for recorders, as well as tuned and untuned percussion and easy parts for clarinet and trumpet.

'Studio Junior Musicpax'   Each **£ 2,3**
Studio Music
- Over seventeen titles in the same format as the Middle Eight kits.

'Top Class'   Each **££ 2,3**
Boosey & Hawkes
- Similar parts to the other kits, but in a card folder. Titles include tunes from *West Side Story*.

'Middle Eight Classical Music Kits'   Each **££ 3,4**

'Middle Eight Original Music Kits'   Each **££ 3,4**

'Middle Eight Medley Music Kits'   Each **££ 3,4**
Boosey & Hawkes
- Plastic packs of a score and enough part for a class or school orchestra. Parts include C and B flat melody and harmony, plus E flat, F, easy B flat, easy violin, viola, bass, percussion and guitar. 'Classical' titles include Elgar, Sousa and Offenbach. 'Original' titles include several Beatles arrangements. 'Medley' titles include Sousa marches and a Carmen selection

'Kaleidoscope'   Each  **££ 3,4**
Music Sales (Chester)
- Over 40 titles in a wide range of styles. There are specific parts for wind, brass, and string ensembles, or combinations from each section. Colourful card folder.

'Flexiband'
Faber Music

Each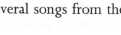

- Similar parts to the Music Kits. Titles include several songs from the show *Cats*.

'Ensemble Microjazz'
Christopher Norton
Boosey & Hawkes

Each

- A series of four titles with two tunes in each, consisting of a short score plus 50 parts including optional vocal parts. The titles are original pieces in jazz style.

'Backing Tracks' 1 and 2
Patrick Dunn
Boosey & Hawkes

Score and cassette

Each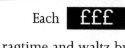

Class set of parts

Each

- An introduction to specific styles such as blues, ragtime and waltz by means of original pieces in three (graded) parts. The recorded backing is on cassette. Useful teaching notes are included.

'Sound Bites'
Barry Russell
Boosey & Hawkes
Bohemia to the Balkans
A Carnival of Carols

Each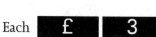

- Classroom projects for mixed ability classes. Each title has four projects exploring a particular style.

Keyboard ensemble

Play Together Levels 1 to 5
Bill Martin
Yamaha/Music Sales (Chester)

Each

- Mixed ability pieces for classroom keyboards.

Switched On!
David Bierman
Oxford University Press
Teacher's book

Three pupils' books	Each	£

- A keyboard course including composing and improvising. The three pupils' books are subtitled 'Tunes to play', 'Shapes and structures', 'Projects and games'.

Books on using electronic technology

As these books become obsolete so quickly, it is best to check current titles in the current British Music Education Yearbook.

Music, plays, cantatas and shows

It is not reasonable to make a selection from the hundreds of titles available. Recommendation from other teachers seems to be the most popular way of choosing a school or class production. The main publishers in this field are: Music Sales, which includes Chester, Novello, Golden Apple, and Shawnee (American); IMP; Weinberger; Universal Edition; Lovely Music (many Jan Holdstock titles); Oxford University Press.

Other sources for information and published material

Local museums, history centres, libraries, cultural groups and professional music groups are a good source of information and practical help. For information on world musics, the Commonwealth Institute, the Horniman Museum, The School of Oriental and African Studies, and WOMAD (World of Music and Dance) are particularly useful. The British Music Education Yearbook lists addresses and contact numbers for many of these organizations.

Your local music shop

Any good music shop should be able to obtain the instruments and publications listed in this chapter. The more you use your local shop, the more likely they are to stock all the material that you would like to be able to see before buying!